▶▶FWD this link

A Rough Guide to staying amused online
when you should be working

www.roughguides.com

Credits

↦FWD this link

Edit, design and layout: Andrew Clare
Illustration: Peter Buckley and Elliot Elam
Cover design: Peter Buckley
Proofreading: Adam Smith
Production: Rebecca Short and Vicky Baldwin

Rough Guides Reference

Editors: Peter Buckley,
Tracy Hopkins, Sean Mahoney,
Matt Milton, Joe Staines, Ruth Tidball
Director: Andrew Lockett

Publishing information

This first edition published September 2008 by Rough Guides Ltd:
80 Strand, London WC2R 0RL
345 Hudson St, 4th Floor, New York 10014, USA
mail@roughguides.com

Distributed by the Penguin Group:
Penguin Books Ltd, 80 Strand, London WC2R 0RL
Penguin Putnam, Inc., 375 Hudson Street, NY 10014, USA
Penguin Group (Australia), 250 Camberwell Road, Camberwell, Victoria 3124, Australia
Penguin Books Canada Ltd, 90 Eglinton Avenue East, Toronto, Ontario, Canada M4P 2YE
Penguin Group (New Zealand), Cnr Rosedale and Airborne Roads, Albany, Auckland, New Zealand

Typeset in Montara, Minion and Helvetica Neue

© Rhodri Marsden, 2008

224 pages; includes index

A catalogue record for this book is available from the British Library.

ISBN: 978-1-84836-019-8

1 3 5 7 9 8 6 4 2

Printed and bound in China

▶▶FWD this link

A Rough Guide to staying amused online
when you should be working

by Rhodri Marsden

www.roughguides.com

Contents

About the author

Rhodri Marsden is under the impression that he is a writer and a musician. He pens features and columns for *The Independent* covering technology and new media issues, and has written about food, music, the Internet and general unusualness for such diverse media outlets as *The Guardian*, *Time Out*, BBC Radio Wales, *The Independent On Sunday* and *The Observer Music Monthly*. Oh, and the *Daily Mail* (once). *Franz Ferdinand* (the band, not the Archduke) described him in *The Guardian* as "one of Britain's leading bloggers", and when not pontificating on his own blog he adds to the digital information mountain by contributing to the *Radio Times* website. He also plays keyboards with Scritti Politti, and is working on a book about the unrelenting tediousness of being in a band on the road. He lives in London and, as you've probably guessed, wrote this glowing biography himself.

Acknowledgements

Thanks to Toby Slater for an invaluable outpouring of ideas which helped get this project in shape, Jenny McIvor for her critical eye and several patient explanations of the difference between "which" and "that", Elliot Elam for illustrations, Peter Buckley for yet more illustrations and commissioning me to write the thing, and Tim Bates for all his support and encouragement. Lastly, thanks to everyone (and, in particular, a consistently benevolent group of bloggers at livejournal.com) who FWD me more links than I know what to do with. This book is dedicated to you, in the forlorn hope that we all stop wasting time on the Internet.

Introduction

It was once said by someone vastly more poetic than myself that "procrastination is the assassin of opportunity". Or, in the kind of language the average boss uses: "Look, if you don't stop messing about on the Internet, you're fired." Anyone who has sat in an Internet cafe and watched their session time-out before they've even got around to checking their email will be familiar with the almost paralyzing effect that an Internet browser can have, dragging you mercilessly across the information superhighway in the search of anything other than actual information. It knows that what you really want is idle distraction. Entertainment. Stupid stuff. Brief moments of titillation, the odd belly laugh, and perhaps a brutal, expletive-ridden online argument for pudding.

Introduction

Of course, you turn on the computer with the best of intentions – perhaps to book a flight or check your bank balance – but instead you find yourself gazing at the lyrics of half-remembered novelty hits from the long, hot summer of 1976, or pictures showing inventive and artistic uses of streaky bacon. We might proudly inform friends that we're at the cutting edge of modern technology, what with our wireless routers, our crystal clear flat-screen monitors and our 20Mbps Internet connections. But what we don't tell them is that we mainly use them to look at pictures of dogs wearing hats.

This aimless, fruitless meandering through cyberspace has been given a name: wilfing. It's an acronym for "what was I looking for?" – a phrase which is subconsciously uttered by thousands of us every minute, as we accidentally become embroiled in a fascinating online trawl of metal detector serial numbers instead of filing our tax returns, or after a whole afternoon of using Google's store of satellite images to hover above Mount Kilimanjaro at two thousand feet, for no other reason than we just can.

This book brings together some of the most popular, notable and ludicrous Internet distractions that have ever conspired to stop us doing things we should really be doing. Of course, friends and relatives constantly email us links that are barely worth clicking on (If your mum has already referred you half a dozen times this month to pictures of kittens rolling about to a tinny musical accompaniment, you probably don't even bother opening her emails any more). But a select few become unstoppable, spreading exponentially among the Internet community, getting picked up by popular websites and kicking off a whole new round of infectious forwarding. The word that's used is "viral". And there's really no better way of describing it.

Any book documenting Internet phenomena couldn't hope to be comprehensive – not least because a galaxy's worth of new data is dumped online every second. During the process of putting this together, I lost count of the number of times that someone said to me something like "hang on, though, you must have seen that amazing video of two drunk Hungarians trying to put a log on the back of a bike". Sometimes I'd seen the thing they were referring to. If I hadn't, more often than not, I'd add it to the list. But the line had to be drawn somewhere. (And, in case you're interested, that line was just in front of the German variety act on YouTube who seemingly produce six-foot long poles from each others' heads. By the time I'd clicked my way through to them, the book was in danger of never being finished.) So the book you currently hold in your hands is, let's say, a representative sample of the kind of things that fill the hours we spend in front of an Internet browser, while a Word document or an Excel spreadsheet lurks resentfully in the background.

Under normal circumstances, the traditional media – TV, radio and print – would be pretty unlikely to champion the work of a drugged-up beatboxer, a skateboarding dog or a man putting an iPod in a blender. But the fact that all three have already achieved prominence on the Internet changes everything. Online popularity somehow validates them; if the general public has voted with its clicking finger, it would almost be negligent of a budding television producer not to fawn over them, wouldn't it? So here are an initial ten links that, if you're a regular Internet timewaster, you couldn't possibly have missed. And even if you don't fritter away your time online, such was their omnipresence that you might well catch yourself thinking "hang on ... haven't I seen these somewhere before?"

Mahir
tinyurl.com/ypgly

If there was ever a moment where it became clear that the Internet had put celebrity status within everyone's reach, it was when Turkish table tennis fan Mahir Çağri became internationally famous, purely through uploading a website that was a bit rubbish. Back in 1999, having a rubbish website wasn't particularly unique, but Mahir rose to the top of the pile with such profound pronouncements as "I have many many music enstrumans my home I can play", "My eyes green … I live alone !!!!!!!!!" and, of course, "I like sex". All this ended up forming the basis of a wildly unsuccessful Christmas single in 2000. (Exercise tolerance and restraint while viewing this promotional video: tinyurl.com/5lujch.)

Tron guy
tronguy.net/TRONcostume

Jay Maynard deeply divided Internet opinion when his valiant attempt at recreating a costume from the Disney sci-fi movie *TRON* started to gain notoriety. Some thought that his commitment to seeing through an essentially pointless craft project should be applauded, even encouraged; others were so deeply appalled by witnessing a balding, overweight man wearing a cream-coloured one-piece jumpsuit that they urged other people to have a look and share their feelings of utter disgust. This perfectly demonstrates a central paradox of the Web; a widely loathed website is a wildly popular website – because the hit counter never lies.

A tragic story: a cat desperately tries to make itself understood to the human race, predicting imminent global catastrophe; we merely laugh and upload the footage to YouTube.

Oh, long johnson
youtube.com/watch?v=ONmhQJy1ViA

By now, this footage of a peculiarly verbose cat is probably a staple of Funniest Animals-style television shows, but the clip owes much of its popularity to the Internet. On this version, the cat's mournful utterances are subtitled; "oh, long johnson" and "oh, don piano" are the most meaningful phrases, if you can believe that. Our enthusiasm for this feline poetry has resulted in the opening of an online store at ohlongjohnson.com, where you can not only buy branded mugs and fridge magnets, but also see a dog suffer the indignity of wearing an outfit that pays tribute to a talking cat.

Janice, it hurts
youtube.com/watch?v=HzS-OdWVpHo

This video taught everyone a valuable lesson: if you're overweight and terrified of heights, don't let a relative persuade you to go on a fairground ride that offers video mementoes of you being shot into the air. Had it only featured the poor boy who ended up with a seatbelt wrapped around his neck, it would probably have languished in obscurity. But there's something

Getting your bookmarks in order

For some people, the Internet provides ephemeral, disposable entertainment. They take a quick look at a page before moving on; they're perfectly happy if they never see it again, and would certainly never dream of storing the link on their computer for posterity. But your Internet browser of choice – Internet Explorer, Firefox, Safari or any number of obscure younger siblings – lets you store bookmarks in a handy menu and, if you're feeling particularly well organized, in folders, subfolders, or subfolders of subfolders. In reality, however, it's a drag to keep these in order, and they usually become stuffed with sites that are not only past their sell-by date, but also prevent you from finding the ones you actually want.

Social bookmarking takes those bookmarks out of the browser and sticks them online to be shared with everyone. Of course, over-active bookmarking will still swamp your account with thousands of sites you may never, ever return to. But the moment you unearth something interesting and make a note of it, it becomes an implicit recommendation for other people to go and have a look. And social bookmarking sites (such as Digg, del.icio.us and many others) are making those email FWDs which gave this book its name much less of a menace by streamlining the process of recommendation. If you feel like being diverted and want something new from the Web, they will give you an instant snapshot of what's popular at that moment.

The absurdly named *del.icio.us* (can you remember where the dots are? I sometimes have trouble) was the first social bookmarking compelling about the contrast between the boy yelling "Stop it! Stop it! It hurts! It hurts! Janice, it hurts!" and Janice herself, who is completely immobilized by helpless laughter and shows not one iota of concern. Hilarious, but somehow chilling.

site to gain widespread popularity: it introduced the concept of tagging, which lets you search for all recommended links that are related to, say, sun dried tomatoes, or Indian cricketer Ravi Shastri. Other sites such as *Reddit*, *Fark*, *Newsvine* and *Digg* use voting systems to show us what's hot and what's merely lukewarm, and the rapid turnover of links makes them essential if you're after up-to-the-minute recommendations. Indeed, such is their power to kickstart virals that every new website is desperate to be Dugg or Farked. (And, annoyingly, people will constantly attempt to craftily market their own creative endeavours by spamming these sites, although vigilant users will do their best to give offenders the thumbs down.)

Stumbleupon, meanwhile, adds a random element to the search for entertainment. The site installs a toolbar in your browser, with which you can give the thumbs-up or the heave-ho to any webpages you come across in the course of your "working" day. But when you're bored of doing that, you can just click the "Stumble" button, sit back, and see which web pages it throws up based on a) users' recommendations and b) the kind of sites you've been rating highly. It also works in tandem with Google, by giving certain pages within search results a sprinkling of gold stars if they've been recommended by Stumblers – a perfect way of picking out the best of the Net while minimizing the impact on your mouse.

With all these communities busy rating websites as they go, it's helping to create a Internet utopia where the good stuff is shared and the rubbish is jettisoned. In theory, it's finely honing the art of aimless browsing – if such a thing isn't a contradiction in terms.

The hampster dance
webhamster.com

Some Internet attractions are so utterly mundane and require so little of us that it's easy to imagine ourselves as goldfish, passively staring out of our bowls and unquestioningly lapping up anything that appears in front of our eyes. This nine-second loop of animated hamsters dancing to a speeded up version of the opening music to Disney's *Robin Hood* wasn't a great cultural achievement, it wasn't funny, it wasn't profound, it neither provoked nor answered any questions – it just sat there. And people – millions of us – watched it. Canadian art student Deidre LaCarte created it, apparently, to see whether she could get more Internet traffic than her friends. She won the bet, despite not being able to spell "hamster".

Miss South Carolina
tinyurl.com/yscpz2

Caitlin Upton was in the running to become Miss Teen USA 2007, right up until the point during the pageant when she was asked why one-fifth of Americans couldn't locate the USA on a map. "I believe that our, uh, education like such as, uh, South Africa and, uh, the Iraq, everywhere like such as, and, I believe that they should, our education over here in the US should help the US, uh, or, uh, should help South Africa and should help the Iraq and the Asian countries, so we will be able to build up our future, for our children," she stated, solemnly. Upton only came fourth, but received colossal international media coverage. Unlike the winner of the competition, who must be kicking herself that she didn't display similar incoherence.

Badgers badgers badgers

weebls-stuff.com/toons/badgers

Jonti Picking probably wasn't aware of the service he was doing for the human race when he created a Flash animation featuring a poisonous mushroom, a slow-moving snake and a group of badgers doing calisthenics (pictured below). In turn, we had no idea quite how we had managed without it. In one of the more surreal moments of demand perfectly meeting supply, Picking's creation was lapped up thirstily by everyone who set eyes on it –

and, strangely, the animal rights organization PETA loved it so much they parodied it for one of their own promotional videos (tinyurl.com/59mkoo).

Badgers badgers badgers badgers badgers badgers badgers – Sure, Steve, I'll have that report with you in ten minutes – badgers badgers badgers badgers badgers badgers badgers.

Bonsai kitten

shorty.com/bonsaikitten

People who believe in UFOs are rigorously scientific sceptics compared to the millions of gullible Web surfers who believed this hoax, which was created by students at Massachussetts Institute Of Technology (MIT). It purports to show the method by which kittens can be grown in glass jars. Kittens, of course, can't be grown in glass jars. But that didn't stop thousands of people getting upset about it, the Humane Society of the United States calling for the site to be removed, and the FBI to launch an investigation. Delight in further hoaxes in chapter 4, and more geeky pranks in chapter 8.

Evolution of dance
youtube.com/watch?v=dMH0bHeiRNg

It's not particularly cutting edge. Just a six-minute comedy routine, with a single camera focused on a bloke wearing jeans and a t-shirt who proceeds to dance his way through fifty years of pop music history. But it's had 85 million views at the time of writing, and may well hit the magic YouTube billion by the time you read this. Its success, like all physical comedy, is that it's universal; we're all aware, for example, of the inherent preposterousness of the "YMCA" dance. Judson Laipply (for it is he) is also a successful motivational speaker; when he posted this video he described it as "The funniest six minutes you will ever see!" – which is proof, if nothing else, of the power of positive thinking.

Subservient chicken
subservientchicken.com

Some poor actor has given the impression of being stuck in a chicken suit for the last four years, responding to requests that bored people type in at the bottom of the browser window. If this were actually the case (rather than being a wildly successful viral for Burger King) it would be almost as demeaning as being stuck in a cage awaiting slaughter. Typing "moonwalk" or "riverdance" will get him gyrating and, should you want him to, he'll demonstrate his golf swing, read a book, turn off the lights or attempt a miserable cartwheel. But if you dare to use offensive language, you will incur the considerable wrath of the chicken. Which isn't a sentence you read every day.

Who, me? 1

- - - - - - - - - - - - - - - -

One moment you're lurking quietly in some undiscovered corner of cyberspace. The next, you're getting calls to come and appear on breakfast television. You might not have any discernible talent other than getting drunk on sherry and stumbling into a nearby cactus plant, but if it entertains people for a few fleeting online moments, you will henceforth be celebrated – at least for the foreseeable future – as Cockeyed Cactus Boy. (Or girl.) (But probably boy.)

Not many of the people behind the links in this book could honestly say that they expected to receive such widespread attention, but this particular group are tied together by the utter shock that they experienced: they were unwillingly pushed into the spotlight at the end of a pointed stick, and left to absorb the full glare of publicity. They may have been snapped or recorded or filmed without their knowledge; or they might vaguely remember someone documenting their special moment but certainly never expected to see or hear it again; or they might have deliberately placed their vignette on a website, never imagining that the general public would be remotely interested in it. But when word gets around on the Internet, man, word really does get around.

The process of "going viral" can be at once exhilarating and terrifying. At its best, it can feel like several hundred people turning up at your house for a surprise birthday party at which they're all going to give you some money and tell you how brilliant you are. Of course, you can't please all of the people all of the time, and inevitably some of the attendees at said party will start to harangue you viciously and pelt you with peanuts – but that's part and parcel of viral fame; you have to take the rough with the smooth, the gr8ters with the h8ters. But at its worst, the party gets horribly out of hand and someone vomits down the back of your sofa. Deliberately. Viral fame can be the most invasive intrusion imaginable – and made all the worse by the fact that, up until that point, the most recognition you'd had in your life was being awarded an iron-on patch for swimming the five-metre width of your local pool.

Most of the following people have emerged unscathed; some have had their lives enriched by their experience; some have even used it to launch alternative careers. But none of them would be quite the same today if it wasn't for the Internet.

The worst driver
youtube.com/
watch?v=7RMLt28n0-M

The Net is rammed with examples of bad driving – a vehicle pulling up at lights with a petrol nozzle still sticking out of the tank, epic parallel parking attempts galore – and men instantly attribute all of these to women drivers, regardless of who might actually be behind the wheel. But the evidence is irrefutable in this clip of a woman overturning her car while trying to drive through a gate that's easily the width of an armoured personnel carrier. After being helped from the vehicle, she quietly walks away in embarrassment, unaware that the whole thing was captured on CCTV.

Peter Oakley
askgeriatric.com

When this self-confessed online video addict posted his first video blog at the age of 78 back in the summer of 2006, he predicted that his clips would largely consist of bitching and grumbling. What he didn't predict was the massive interest his clips would generate among the online community, which was delighted that someone of Oakley's age was getting to grips with a webcam. Today, he's still in the top 30 most subscribed YouTube channels worldwide, and has become the spearhead of a movement – Silver Surfers – to encourage older people to get online.

World's worst burglar
youtube.com/watch?v=c3aYZQJZ1SQ

Burglars, for obvious reasons, generally try to keep their exploits a secret. This particular guy, however, became internationally famous and had to suffer the indignity of being called a "dumbass" by a few thousand online jurors after CCTV footage of his bungled break-in became an online hit. We witness him having trouble climbing into a grocery store, then crashing into shelves of ketchup, failing to locate anything worth stealing and, crucially, becoming trapped in the building. Managing to light up a stress-relieving cigarette is his one successful act during the whole disastrous episode.

Afro ninja
youtube.com/watch?v=6njscWrdnM0

They didn't believe David when he claimed that he could kill Goliath, and few believed this group of budding young actors when they turned up at an audition claiming that they were action hero material. The difference is, of course, that David did manage to kill Goliath, while these actors just managed to end up looking a bit stupid. But they did ensure that phrases

such as "I'll show you tough", "I never lose", and "I hope you like pain" would go down in comedy history. Incredibly, the "Afro Ninja" who badly mistimes his backflip – stuntman Mark Hicks – is working on a full-length film based on his thirteen seconds of Internet infamy.

Party-mad Corey Worthington stubbornly refuses to remove his sunglasses, in spite of – or perhaps because of – a stern admonishment from newsreader Leila McKinnon.

Corey Worthington, party liaison
youtube.com/watch?v=X2EDtxEumFl

Most sixteen-year-olds will return home from a party with a sullenly recounted tale of how it was "alright" and that "not much happened". But the 500 Melbourne teenagers who attended a house party organized by Corey Worthington while his parents were on holiday found themselves swooped down upon by police helicopters after events got out of control. Worthington subsequently appeared on an Australian news show to face a dressing down from presenter Leila McKinnon, but somehow managed to emerge the victor. "Take a long, hard look at yourself," she said. "I have," he replied. "Everyone has, they love it."

Baby shower

There's one Internet attraction that guarantees to entertain more than any other. Irrespective of your taste in music or your attitude towards surreal comedy, regardless of whether you're high on life or you're coming to terms with having your car stolen, this clip of a baby laughing (*youtube.com/watch?v=5P6UU6m3cqk*) seems to be the universal panacea. It just makes absolutely everything seem okay.

Who knows why the film industry invests such huge sums in big names, elaborate sets and special effects when it could happily entertain forty million people with a video of a man saying "Ping!" or, alternatively, "Plong!" to his child, and the baby responding with unrestrained glee. You may imagine that a video of quadruplets up to a similar gambit (*youtube.com/watch?v=GwriOyQf1EA*) would provide four times the amusement, but it doesn't quite hit the finely honed simplicity of the first.

Of course, if you've got a child of your own and you've had enough of the giggling, squealing and crying, you may find solace in the otherworldly mysticism of the Karate Baby (*youtube.com/watch?v=iasgZ5uFLGE*) – although his profound wisdom probably won't be revealed to us until he's at least out of nappies.

The Saugeen stripper
everything2.com/index.pl?node_id=1784779

Breaking news: there's no shortage of nudity online. Strange, then, that one of the more benign examples – of a young woman performing a striptease on a college campus – should have created such a buzz on the Internet. University officials were upset when the reputation of their seat of learning as a "party school" was further tarnished by these pictures – but the main reason for its popularity was disbelief on the part of the viewer: most graduates' memories of university involve a) writing essays and b) wishing that someone – anyone! – would come and cavort naked in their immediate vicinity.

Pub trapdoor
youtube.com/watch?v=Hz355d7HUBw

There's no purer form of slapstick than someone disappearing feet first down a hole. The competition is stiff – getting a pie in the face, being hit by a ladder as the person carrying it turns through 180° – but the absent floor will always guarantee a belly laugh. Thanks once again to the placement of a CCTV camera to deter burglars, we get to see a Scottish barmaid – oblivious to the fact that a trapdoor behind her has just been opened – take a step backwards and disappear. Fortunately, she recovered sufficiently to be able to recount her admittedly short story on the American chatshow circuit.

My god, we're going viral

For many people, the first sign that they're experiencing a fleeting moment of Internet fame is that their website stops working. While the major sites that we use every day are hooked up to the Internet by means of inconceivably huge data pipes that are probably the width of the Grand Canyon, our own creations that cost us a few dollars a month to have hosted merely share a feeble, spindly connection with several others; the hosting company is only really able to offer you such a cheap deal on the understanding that barely anyone will want to look at your website. On a day-to-day basis, this rarely presents any problems: the Internet is the ultimate home of vanity publishing, and the majority of traffic your website gets will generally be down to you checking to see how much traffic your website is getting.

But then you go viral. Let's imagine that you've just created a page on your website featuring a picture of you eating blancmange while perched at the top of a motorcycle pyramid. (Hey, it can happen.) This unusual spectacle might have all the makings of a viral hit – particularly if you weren't aware that your trousers were falling down when the picture was taken. So, let's say that you forward that link to thirty friends, and that half of them forward it to thirty of their friends, and half of those people forward it to thirty of their friends, too – already a grand total of 6750 inquisitive clickers. If the picture is a hi-res JPG – let's say 450Kb in size – you'll have already shifted well over 3Gb of data in a relatively short space of time. Whoever's hosting your website in exchange for peanuts will already be raising their eyebrows, and probably preparing to fire off a warning email about exceeding your bandwidth limits.

If your page is then linked to from *digg.com* (you've been dugg), or *fark.com* (farked), or *Metafilter* (mefried), or *slashdot.org* (slashdotted) or *stumbleupon.com* (stumbled), then you could be dealing with tens of thousands or even hundreds of thousands of visitors before lunchtime. But while you're punching the air, thrilled that the recognition that has eluded you for so many years has finally arrived – albeit because you ate blancmange in an unusual location – it's your hosting provider's worst nightmare. And more often than not, they'll just shut you down, leaving you to weep into your keyboard and dream of what might have been.

Of course, if your picture is hosted with a massive online service such as Flickr, you won't have this problem. Flickr (owned by Yahoo!) will barely register this sudden interest in your antics from your new-found global audience. And if your video is hosted with a site like YouTube (owned by Google) you can just sit back, safe in the knowledge that your video won't suddenly disappear at an inconvenient moment, and watch the number of visitors go up, and up, and up. Just imagine: you, making a profound, blancmange-based connection with thousands upon thousands of people across the globe. If you never truly understood what the word exponential means, going viral will make it crystal clear. But don't go booking your world tour just yet – remember that tomorrow, they'll all have gone somewhere else, and you'll be pretty much forgotten. Tragic, isn't it.

Boom goes the dynamite
youtube.com/watch?v=W45DRy7M1no

It has all the makings of a heroic story: the sports anchor on a student-run TV news programme drops out at the last minute, leaving plucky Brian Collins to don a jacket and tie and step in – and, who knows, maybe kick-start a glittering television career. Unfortunately it didn't quite work out like that: autocue

trouble left Collins gasping in panic and frustration while footage of a basketball match rolled. Eventually he abandoned the script, and when two points were scored he shouted "boom goes the dynamite!" – which ended up becoming a catchphrase employed by sports commentators across the US.

Crazy Dave
video.google.com/videoplay?docid=-6266680493612337181

Overtaking your father on a main road runs completely contrary to the accepted order of things; Dad has earned the right to dictate the speed of your convoy over several years of nappy changing, handing out pocket money and putting up with teenage tantrums. Dave Mills, however, intensely frustrated with the speed of his dad's tractor, gives an ear-splitting running commentary on his overtaking manoeuvre, from "I think he knows what's coming!" to "He did not look happy!". As a result, Dave's road skills became the toast of British TV show *Soccer AM*.

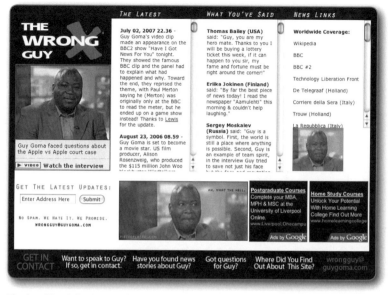

Thanks to his website, Guy Goma's moment in the spotlight has been extended into a multi-faceted multimedia experience.

Guy Goma

guygoma.com

In a case of literally getting the wrong Guy, the BBC succeeded in grilling Guy Goma – an applicant for an entry-level IT job – on its 24-hour rolling news channel, in the mistaken belief that he was Guy Kewney, a technology expert who was in fact sitting in the reception area watching the fiasco unfold on a nearby television set. Goma, perhaps believing that he was undergoing some kind of initiative test, struggled manfully and in broken English with the questions: "So … a big surprise anyway," he improvised, vaguely. The BBC didn't reward him with any kind of job – but he quickly became a cult hero.

Who, me?

"I'm having the time of my life, and I've never felt this way before ... mainly because I've never been hoisted in the air while wearing a bridal gown." Those hallmark moves from the finale of Dirty Dancing were given a new spin in this incredibly popular wedding video.

Dirty dancing
youtube.com/watch?v=ZYhlm9GTAQ0

The announcement of the first dance at any normal wedding is generally a cue for a sheepish bride and groom to shuffle awkwardly around a polished floor to the sound of Whitney Houston's "I Will Always Love You", unaware that it's actually a song about a cataclysmic relationship breakdown. Not so at the wedding of Julia Boggio and James Derbyshire; they considered which film sequence they could pastiche, ruled out the funeral scene in *Ghandi* and the destruction of the Death Star, and wisely plumped for the climax of *Dirty Dancing*. Not a dry eye was left on YouTube as a result.

Mother Goose
chumfm.com/MorningShow/bits/march24.swf

While leaving a voicemail message for his boss a Texan construction manager witnessed a man drive through a red light and collide with a car containing four elderly ladies. When the offending driver leapt out of his car to protest his innocence, the women subjected him to a brutal assault with pepper spray, umbrellas and handbags, according to the vivid description of the construction manager – who, by this point, has become hysterical with laughter. "HAHA! She's hitting him with a BIBLE!" he screams, much to our delight.

Hidden talents

Fanny farting
youtube.com/watch?v=Wm0gXrjCreo

We men have been laughing at each others' farts since well before the invention of the wheel. But women, perhaps enticed by the side benefit of achieving some kind of notoriety, have been rising to the challenge of emulating our gaseous achievements and sharing the evidence with the world. Here, our heroine strikes a blow for the equality of the sexes by producing rasping sounds from down below at will. It's telling that few men express any kind of disgust in the comments underneath the video, probably figuring that keeping shtum will secure them the moral right to break wind whenever they like.

I wish the Internet had never happened

Islamic Rage Boy

Shakeel Bhat was an unassuming chap living a fairly unremarkable life in Kashmir. His one indulgence was attending protest marches to chant slogans against Indian occupation, and against anti-Islamic sentiment in general. But unfortunately for Bhat, when he chants, he looks angry. I mean, ferociously angry. Images of his blind fury strewn across cyberspace have made him synonymous with Muslim anger towards the west – and today he's simply known as Islamic Rage Boy (*thenoseonyourface.com/category/islamic-rage-boy*). "There but for the grace of god," you might think, recalling the time you dished out a torrent of abuse to a traffic warden but luckily didn't end up with your contorted expression splashed across the global media. But for Bhat, it's too late; he's already become a global hate figure. In an interview with the *Daily Mail* he was quoted as saying "I surely get hurt when I see these pictures. This is terrorism for me."

Star Wars Kid

The problem with viral Internet fame is that once you're out there, there's no clawing your way back to anonymity. This was certainly the case with the French Canadian teenager who became known to the world as the Star Wars Kid (*youtube.com/watch?v=HPPj6vilBmU*), and whose video still solicits hourly comments several years after it first came to prominence. "I want my life back," he was quoted as saying, after footage of him pretending to engage in futuristic lightsaber combat using a golf ball retriever became the most popular viral video of all time. When he set up that video camera in a studio at his school and decided to imitate Darth Maul for a few moments, there was no way he could have known the consequences of giving his friends a copy. But that copy became five copies, and via filesharing networks became dozens, then hundreds, and then thousands – and now it's been watched over a billion times in its various forms. Of course, many of us simply found the Star Wars Kid charming; anyone who has sung into a hairbrush pretending to be a pop star can easily identify with his moment of boredom-fuelled madness. But on the World Wide Web it's the voices of derision that are heard loudest – and for an anonymous chubby boy who never sought any attention, that's going to hurt.

Little Fatty

Another plump teenager from China who is now known as Little Fatty (or Xiao Pang in Chinese) would also have sued, had he known who on earth to slap the lawsuit on. A photo of him looking sideways at the camera during a road safety lesson ended up becoming raw material for thousands of Photoshop experiments; overwhelmed by his new-found fame and unable to take legal action, Little Fatty – real name Qian Zhijun – took the only option available: a pragmatic attempt to turn the infamy to his advantage by launching his own website (*xiaopang.cn*) in the hope of making some money. Another reluctant Internet star is American Gary Brolsma: he filmed himself miming to a Moldovan pop song (*youtube.com/watch?v=60og9gwKh1o*) and in doing so created the second most popular viral video ever, tucked in behind the Star Wars Kid. Again, Brolsma wasn't trying to amuse anyone apart from himself. "I'm just a regular guy," he said, "who sits in front of his computer bored out of his mind and messing around on the Internet." You're not alone, Gary. But I don't think I'll be uploading videos of myself miming to any Girls Aloud records. Just in case.

Star Wars trumpet solo

youtube.com/watch?v=Wffwg7pA0t8

Stacey Hedger, winner of a 1993 beauty pageant in Douglas, Arizona, went forward to the state finals with the dream of eventually becoming Miss America. When it came to the "talent" section of the show, she put on a glittery costume, picked up her trumpet, and played along to the *Star Wars* theme tune. Whether Stacey was out of tune with the music or vice versa is irrelevant; the resulting video of her performance redefined the phrase "toe curling". Until she was tracked down in late 2007 Stacey had no idea of her online infamy, but she now says that her family think it's the "greatest thing in the world".

Matt Harding's exuberant tourism brought the awkward gyrations of the white, Western male to a global audience: citizens of Dubai, Chuuk, Palau, Norway and Rwanda found themselves delighted at his efforts, if somewhat unimpressed by his jigging, more often than not, as seen here, observed from an unsettling distance.

Where the hell is Matt?

wherethehellismatt.com

Matt Harding will never win awards for choreography: his dancing resembles someone trying to run away from a milk float while being held back by an invisible elastic band. But after having boogied energetically in several exotic global destinations during 2005 and uploaded the resulting videos, he became another unlikely Internet celebrity. The following year, a brand of chewing gum paid for him to repeat the escapade in a new set of locations, and at the time of writing he's still frugging awkwardly around the planet to some frenzied, incessant beat that's audible only to Matt himself.

David "Elsewhere" Bernal

youtube.com/watch?v=HSoVKUVOnfQ

It's a home video of a low-key Korean-American talent show back in 2001. A couple of ambitious young robotic dancers make an unremarkable attempt at emulating androids, before the unassuming figure of David Bernal mooches onto the stage. The next sixty seconds of footage were to change his life: as his arms and legs slide about like troublesome tagliatelle the audience screams in disbelief, and advertising executives watching the clip on the Internet lick the end of their pencils and jot down his name. Bernal's liquid limbs have since appeared in ads for Volkswagen, Apple and Pepsi.

I've not touched a drop

Drunk driver
youtube.com/watch?v=U1VmGjJJFrc

For anyone trying to prove to a police officer that they're not drunk, complying with a request to produce a driving license should prove to be the least of their problems. Not so for this gentleman, who struggles to locate it, then drops his wallet, and in an attempt to bend over and retrieve it succeeds only in staggering headfirst into a wall, leaving a cranium shaped indentation. The policeman in charge seems strangely sympathetic to the man's plight, responding to his second crash-landing with the phrase "you're going to have to stop doing that, you know."

Can't get up
youtube.com/watch?v=qM6vzMpf-GI

Most of us are aware that the earth rotates at about a thousand miles per hour, while simultaneously orbiting the sun at an even faster speed. Fortunately, these are just facts lobbed at us in geography lessons and don't impair our sense of balance – but not for this poor gentleman, whose affection for the bottle has left him unable to cope with gravity. You almost feel queasy watching him during this four-minute attempt to move across a few paving slabs; the reassuring stability of a nearby hedge offers him some temporary respite, but you do get the feeling that he might still be hanging on to it even today.

Log on bike
youtube.com/watch?v=AKaR5nJg-qo

While alcohol might impair your judgement, depress your mood and occasionally spoil your best trousers, it can boost levels of perseverance and determination to superhuman levels. This wonderful footage of two absolutely hammered Hungarian men attempting – for some unknown reason – to get a log onto the back of a bicycle is made all the more exquisite by the cameraman's inability to stifle his giggles. The moment where one of them decides to take off his shirt – again, for no apparent reason – must rank up there with the classic moments of modern cinema.

Drunken coal miner
youtube.com/watch?v=yhuNKKO4OTE

The humour value of this clip of a drunken Russian coal miner has been ratcheted up by rumours that the television interview taking place in the foreground contains a denial by an official union spokesperson that his workers were drinking on the job. Sadly that's not the case – he's just complaining about them not being paid – but the poverty-stricken miners still clearly have access to cheap, potato based spirits: by lurching backwards and forwards in the middle distance with a face spattered with mud, our hero has allowed alcoholics worldwide to say "well … at least I'm not that bad."

I'm gonna make me 2 a star

- - - - - - - - - - - - - - -

Anyone who has embarked on a creative endeavour will know that getting people to pay any attention is by far the most gruelling and soul-destroying part of any project. Before the Internet, access routes to the general public were tightly controlled by a powerful and disapproving cabal of publishers, record labels, TV and radio producers and the like, and success depended on persuading these people that your work was of sufficient worth. Thousands if not millions would try and fail and, rather than re-experience the pain of rejection, they'd give up. This powerfully effective filter saw unpublished novels gathering dust on top of wardrobes, piles of unsold CDs propping up furniture and finely honed comedy routines abandoned after another

failed attempt by Robin Ribtickle to get a gig at his local pub. Okay, Robin might well have been rubbish. But the public never really got to deliver their judgement on the poor chap.

Today, things are very different. Of course, traditional media still has those tight controls in place that stubbornly prevent, say, my mate Jeff from getting his own primetime Saturday evening chat show. But the Web now offers an alternative channel, a completely unfiltered medium where no one can stop you from unleashing your creative potential. Sure, they can leave abusive comments urging you to stop immediately, but they can't stop you putting it out there. In fact, publishing your own text, audio or video has become so easy that the problem of not being heard has taken on a completely contrasting character: the resulting ocean of new media is so colossal that it's difficult to stop your own effort bobbing over the horizon and out of sight.

Unlike the characters in our last chapter, this lot are the show-offs, the ones waving frantically and shouting "look at me!". They're either getting their hands dirty exploiting the potential of the Net to the full or, at the very least, thankfully accepting all the attention that the Web has pushed their way. Why this motley bunch actually rose to the top is hard to say; there's no well oiled publicity machine at work, here, it's all down to a far more random word-of-mouth process. You might think that they have no talent, or alternatively, you might wonder why on earth they're not yet global megastars. But they've all got where they are today by refreshingly honest means – no backhanders, no pulling favours, no powerful relatives having a quiet word in someone's ear – they've simply managed to catch the ever roving eyes of Internet users worldwide. They may not have achieved fortune, but fame? They have it comfortably in the bag.

Political incorrectness gone mad: The Little superstar video finally made it acceptable for the whole world to unashamedly enjoy the antics of a bodypopping dwarf.

Little superstar
youtube.com/watch?v=gx-NLPH8JeM

It's the sheer impossibility of making any sense of this clip that has made it so incredibly popular. A Tamil dwarf performs some amateurish bodypopping to a cassette of a novelty Madonna cover version by a Dutch rapper, while one of the most bankable stars in Bollywood reclines on a bench, starting and stopping the tape at random. While Indian films are known for their forays into inexplicable surreality, this clip has a particularly hypnotic quality of its own. "I could watch this all day," reads one of the many thousands of comments from entranced viewers.

How much is inside?
cockeyed.com/inside/howmuchinside

I've never spent a single moment wondering how big a briefcase you'd need to hold a million dollars. Nor how many square inches of a human face can be covered by a single Lancôme lipstick, or indeed how many celery stalks could be filled using a regular jar of peanut butter. That doesn't mean, however, that I'm not interested in the results of these cutting-edge experiments – and judging by the continuing popularity of Rob Cockerham's website, we're all fascinated by things that we never imagined we'd be fascinated by.

One red paperclip
oneredpaperclip.blogspot.com

When two people decide to swap one item for another, they both think that they're coming away with the better deal. You could point at any object in your home, right now, and there'll be someone in the world, somewhere, who'll want it more than you do, and would be able to make you a tempting offer for it. It was that bartering instinct that inspired Kyle McDonald to invite offers for his red paperclip; within a year he had swapped his way through pens, campstoves and snow globes to end up with, would you believe, a two storey farmhouse in Saskatchewan.

Jumpstyle duo
youtube.com/
watch?v=tyAvaLsLFl8

You've seen the Argentine tango, right? It's a dramatic, elegant dance where the passionate embrace of a couple evokes a thrilling atmosphere of sexual tension and desire. Here, however, we have jumpstyle, where two blokes in jeans and sneakers hop up and down in unison to the relentless synthesizer stabs and drum machines of Dutch hardcore techno, looking for all the world like a couple of robotic cossack dancers. The top rated tango video on YouTube: 1.8 million views. The top rated jumpstyle video on YouTube: 14 million. It's official – romance is dead.

The Julie/Julia project
http://blogs.salon.com/0001399

Later in the chapter we'll see a group of bloggers whose indiscreet Internet activity led to them being sacked and, as a result, receiving a whole heap of publicity that propelled them to fame. But then there are the bloggers who hit the big time purely because a) they had a good idea, and b) they can write. Julie Powell, stuck in a dead-end secretarial job, spent one year cooking all 536 recipes in the acclaimed 1961 book *Mastering The Art Of French Cooking* by American chef and TV personality Julia Child – and detailed all the sautéing and deglazing on her blog. It's now being madeinto a movie starring Meryl Streep.

Best card trick in the world
youtube.com/watch?v=2KrdBUFeFtY

By any criteria, this isn't really the best card trick in the world. The presentation leaves something to be desired – empty beer cans and stationery littering the desk – and his sleight-of-hand technique comes under fire in the comments section. "I've learned better tricks from drunks in no name bars," says one uncharitable soul. But by calling the video "Best Card Trick In The World," the magic of the Internet search engine made it a self-fulfilling prophecy: anyone searching for the best card trick in the world – some 8.5m and counting – will end up right here.

Cup stacking
youtube.com/watch?v=xNG3sgk02Lc

Here's an arcane pastime, but one that's being rolled out in primary schools all over Europe and America in order to instil some hand-eye coordination skills in our increasingly slothful kids. The knack of speedily and noisily stacking plastic cups into pyramids only comes after weeks of practice – and, no doubt, much hollering from parents in the next room to "stop playing with those bloody cups". But here we see Emily Fox establish a world speed record for cup stacking: no packed stadium, no tickertape – just her, a couple of mates, a school sports hall and a slightly confused parent wondering what's going on.

Back dorm boys
youtube.com/watch?v=N2rZxCrb7iU

We tend not to view the art of lip-synching as one that requires any particular talent. If popstars do it, we accuse them of not being able to sing. If someone catches us doing it while we're jumping up and down on the bed and gyrating provocatively, we're subjected to sneering derision. But two enterprising Chinese sculpture graduates have managed to turn it into a career, their mute interpretations of pop tunes securing a worldwide audience and sponsorship galore. However, the real star has to be their enigmatic friend who sits in the background of all the videos, wisely facing the opposite direction.

Hitch50
hitch50.com

Navigating one's way through the daily torrent of several million bloggers' moribund routines can be tough going. So it's no wonder we adore the ones who are actually on some kind of mission, who tell a story that has both a structure and a potential endpoint. In this story, two guys with the somewhat dog-like names of Scotty and Fiddy succeeded in hitchhiking to all fifty US state capitals in fifty days – and yes, that includes Alaska and Hawaii – without paying for any transport whatsoever. Even more incredibly, their story isn't being made into a film.

You might think that merely hitchhiking across town is fraught with danger, intrigue and unsavoury characters – but, as this elegant site recounts, Scott and Fiddy criss-crossed an entire continent in 50 days, just using their thumbs.

Worst video of all time
youtube.com/watch?v=244qR7SvvX0

This audacious experiment to create the lowest rated video of all time on YouTube ended up succeeding beyond expectations; not only is it officially the worst video – with over 65,000 one-star ratings – but it's also the fourth most viewed video of all time on the site. Not that YouTube are particularly willing to advertise the fact; for some reason this six-second glimpse of the vague outline of Britney Spears somewhere in the middle distance by a hotel pool in Beverly Hills doesn't appear in their official chart rundown. If you haven't seen this, you aren't missing anything. If you have, it's partly your fault that it's so popular.

Noah's daily photo
youtube.com/watch?v=6B26asyGKDo

Much copied since its original posting online, this piece by photographer Noah Kalina was made by taking a snapshot of himself every day over a six-year period, and assembling the resulting pictures as an animation over a moody piano soundtrack. It made for an eerie and somewhat melancholy reminder of our own mortality, while also giving us a pretty good idea of how much Noah will have spent on haircuts during that time. Today, looking a little more haggard than in his student days, he's still taking daily pictures of himself – and has had the honour of his work being parodied in an episode of *The Simpsons*.

"Excuse me – could you tell me which is the right platform for Noroton Heights? Excuse me? Hello?" Improv Everywhere's prank made commuting even more disorientating.

Frozen Grand Central
youtube.com/watch?v=jwMj3PJDxuo

We'll look at more pranks in the next chapter, but this supremely organized group known as Improv Everywhere have become renowned for creating scenes of chaos and confusion. From a man pretending to be Ben Folds in a New York nightclub, to the recreation of a suicide jump off a ledge that's four feet from the ground, Improv Everywhere's team of self-styled "undercover agents" are not only wonderfully imaginative, but also great actors. This stunt has a simple premise: two hundred agents suddenly freeze like statues on the concourse of Grand Central station, provoking anxiety among commuters who fear that they might be next.

I'm gonna make me a star

"Stretch, 2, 3, 4 – and turn, 2, 3, 4 – let me see you move, let me see you groove, let me see you serve a ten-year stretch for armed robbery." Phillippine prisoners emulate Michael Jackson in order to take the edge off another day behind bars.

Prison thriller
youtube.com/watch?v=hMnk7lh9M3o

Opinion is split over the form of punishment meted out to the inmates of the Cebu Provincial Detention and Rehabilitation Center in the Phillippines. It consists of compulsory dance classes, with the results posted on the Internet by a security consultant at the prison. More liberal Internet users believe that their treatment is humiliating and inhumane; this in turn irritates the hell out of those who believe that prison shouldn't be a place where you get to prance around to pop music. But whatever your viewpoint, this recreation of Michael Jackson's "Thriller" is one of the most striking and memorable Internet virals.

Musical shenanigans

It's neither original nor profound to point out that the Internet has revolutionized the process of making, distributing and publicising your music. While you'd previously have had to fork out huge sums for publicists in order to persuade tastemakers in the media to give you a column inch or a minute of airtime, today you can make a record or a video in your bedroom and have it up on the Net within minutes. And, if you're lucky enough to satisfy the ever changing whims of the general public, you might just have a viral hit on your hands. Having said that, it's impossible to know exactly why these videos catch on. Sometimes they're unquestionably brilliant. Sometimes they're unrelentingly terrible. And sometimes there's a mystical secret ingredient that just propels it from inbox to inbox, from blog to blog. Do many people buy the music? Not really. But millions upon millions have heard it.

Canon rock
youtube.com/
watch?v=QjA5faZF1A8

As this clip illustrates, there's only one officially sanctioned way to demonstrate your virtuoso skills on the electric guitar these days: sit on the edge of your bed and thrash your way through a version of Pachelbel's *Canon* as fast as humanly possible. (You might not think you know Pachelbel's *Canon*, but you probably do.) Our baseball hat-wearing friend, here, has already accrued over 42 million hits on YouTube – but dozens of wannabe rock stars have had a go and, with advances in audio technology, they can all recreate the sound of a 200W Marshall amp cranked up to the max at Madison Square Garden. Not like the old days, when playing an electric guitar in your room sounded like spaghetti being plucked with a hard boiled egg.

I'm gonna make me a star

OK Go

youtube.com/
watch?v=pv5zWaTEVkl

Music videos have traditionally attempted to impress with lavish locations and special effects. Like, for example, the singer of Spandau Ballet being teleported from the beach of an idyllic desert island to the crater-strewn surface of a distant planet while drinking a martini. But OK Go gave a perfect demonstration of how magnificent promo videos can be made with no money – much to the chagrin of the professionals. It's just four blokes with no discernible dancing talent jumping in sync on a load of treadmills. As a result, sales of treadmills have, er, remained fairly static.

Hannes Coetzee

youtube.com/watch?v=78VdQuhTdZw

The lazy option for a guitarist is to strum or pick at the instrument while singing or whistling the tune. But that's hardly pushing back musical boundaries. Mr Coetzee, however, picks out the melody on the same instrument by wedging a teaspoon in his mouth and using the curved surface to play on the fretboard. It looks ridiculous, and it probably isn't doing his teeth any favours – but the Internet's appreciation of such a bizarre talent knows no bounds. A vigilant copyright holder keeps having Coetzee's videos taken down, but you should be able to find him somewhere, if you look hard enough.

Getu Hirpo new sound
getuhirpo.com

One of the massive drawbacks of the availability of cheap and user-friendly recording technology is that human beings will insist on buying it, using it, and inflicting the results on the rest of us. I've often proposed a repressive system where people have to prove their talent to a stern panel of judges before they're allowed to record anything, but no-one listens to me. Least of all Mr Hirpo, whose incredibly *laissez faire* attitude to melody and song structure provokes laughter in even the artist himself. "Getu Hirpo has not been discovered by the music industry yet," reads his website, with a heart-rending note of optimism.

Reh Dogg
youtube.com/watch?v=8mWW6kRITEY

On the surface, Reh Dogg has all the attributes of a successful rap artiste. He's got the gold teeth, he's got the menacing sneer, and he's certainly got the uncompromising attitude: "Love me or hate me," he says, "I grow on you like maggots in the trash." But from the opening bars of "Why Must I Cry", you get the feeling that something's not quite right. It might be the way he's soaping himself up in the shower. Or running around aimlessly in the woods, or pointing a gun at his head. But it's mainly his haunting, primal wail. And I don't mean haunting in a good way – not like, er, "Candle In The Wind", dear me, no.

Getting a video online

Anything written about the boom in online video inevitably concludes that the future of broadcasting lies in consumer-created content. But as the majority of home-produced material on the Internet currently consists of woozy footage of birthday presents being unwrapped, it's surely the duty of all netizens to get themselves a YouTube account and start improving the situation.

Your channel is automatically created when you sign up to the site, and subscribers to your channel are notified whenever you upload new video content. This effectively gives you your own show – daily, weekly, it's up to you – and one which people will have difficulty missing, as it's always online and ready to watch. The ability to post videos in response to other people's has had the side effect of creating video blogging communities; if you disagree with someone's opinion on, say, the best celebrity chef, you can deliver your earnest rebuttal and your unconditional love for Nigella Lawson almost in person, and almost face to face.

Your first step is to transfer movie footage from your camera, camcorder or mobile phone to a computer and edit it (if necessary) using software such as iMovie for the Mac, or MovieMaker for PC. The world of video encodings and file formats is awash with complex jargon such as H.264 and XviD, but it's a black art you don't really need to worry about. YouTube seems to be able to deal with whatever you throw at it, and if you keep the size of your finished video to 320x240 pixels, you should be fine. The question of what you're allowed to post isn't so straightforward: YouTube has community-driven policing which certainly works well for content that might be pornographic, defamatory or racially offensive – but, as you'll no doubt be aware, it's pretty ineffective for material that is already copyrighted, despite prominent warnings on the site.

iMovie even lets you export your films and upload them to a YouTube account in one fell swoop.

Promoting your videos can be helped by accurate tagging so they appear prominently in search results; for example, the tags you assign to a film of your cat sliding off a wet conservatory roof might be "cat, roof, slide, hilarious, laughter". Your efforts can be rated by viewers and, if comments are enabled, you can get instant feedback – although sensitive souls who respond poorly to criticism can always turn this feature off. If you're more secretive about your creative endeavours, you can restrict distribution to particular users on the site, and you can always remove the video altogether with a single click; but remember, there are third-party tools available which allow people to download YouTube videos to their hard drive. Your consolation is that the quality is sufficiently grainy to prohibit them from being given a nationwide cinema release…

If your filmmaking ambitions start to flower, sites like Atom Films, GoFish and Youare.tv are encouraging users to produce longer, higher quality videos which, they hope, will rival content produced by big media companies. See here (*tinyurl.com/2wtedd*) for a perfect example of a low-budget animation grabbing international recognition.

Michael Jackson, Malaysian Idol

youtube.com/watch?v=YNatqCzF_Ns

Television shows such as *X Factor* take great delight in presenting us with a slew of young hopefuls who, either through parental encouragement or misplaced self-belief, think that they have a chance of fame. Most of them are consigned to the waste heap after delivering a lacklustre pop song rendition with all the vavoom of Tupperware – but occasionally, you get people who have the ability to shock with their colossal effort coupled with minuscule talent. They were never quietly taken to one side and given an honest appraisal, so they ended up on TV. Ladies and gentlemen, we give you "the worst impersonator in the world".

Icy Spicy Leoncie

youtube.com/user/IcySpicyLeoncie

"Leoncie is like a Fiery Sauce of Ripe Goan Chillies and an Exciting kick of Strong Goan Cashew Feni," says Leoncie. "A Lovely Range of Aggressive and yet Sensual, Dynamic Melodies that touch your Soul." Oh, Leoncie. Her music is undeniably rotten, but I find her enthusiasm utterly adorable. Who couldn't love a woman who writes a song called "Radio Rapist", without imagining for a second that it might be offensive? But it's the upbeat, frisky beat of "Killer In The Park", a carnivalesque spin on the subject of innocent joggers being murdered, that will stick with you and wake you up, screaming, at 3am.

Chocolate Rain

youtube.com/watch?v=EwTZ2xpQwpA

In a parallel universe, Tay Zonday would be as popular and successful as George Michael, Prince, or Elton John. He's a talented keyboard player who has never sought refuge in playing the slow and easy stuff, and has an astonishing baritone voice. But the overall effect is utterly disorientating. It's hard to put a finger on why he's destined to be a curiosity rather than a multi-million selling popstar – but having become the most popular DIY artiste on YouTube by simply filming himself with a pair of headphones on, Mr Zonday's probably not bothering to analyse it. So why should we?

Blogging and getting sacked

The potential of the Internet to eat away at working hours, slash productivity and plunge businesses into the red is something we'll look at more closely in a later chapter. But while many people will have had the experience of being hauled in for a disciplinary and having their wrists slapped for the excessive time they've spent poking people on Facebook or correcting The Libertines' discography on Wikipedia, their embarrassment rarely extends beyond the four walls of Human Resources. The following bloggers, however, were given their marching orders not necessarily for wasting time that should have been allotted to spreadsheet design, but for the more nebulous offence of bringing the name of the company they were working for into disrepute. All originally anonymous, they never identified their employers or work colleagues by name, and most would say that the anecdotes they retold were harmless tales of everyday life. But the data trail they left contained enough references to colleagues' body odour or filthy habits to lead directly back to their desks. Fortunately, the publicity they gained from their sackings brought attention to their writing talent, and all of them are still flourishing today – either as accomplished bloggers, fully fledged authors, or both.

Dooce
dooce.com

Heather Armstrong was working in, as she described it, a "cold dark office" when her blogging activities were rumbled by her employer in early 2002 – well before the word "blog" had entered common parlance, and when she was still writing about life as a single woman in Los Angeles (now she's married with kids in Salt Lake City). Offended by her workplace caricatures, her employers marched her to her car with the contents of her desk in a box and told her never to return. Today, the name of her blog is synonymous with being sacked for blogging ("I've been dooced!") and she has gone on to win several awards for her writing. And, indeed, discreet plaudits from the employers who sacked her in the first place.

Dooced! It's never a good idea to indiscreetly bitch about your work colleagues in public, but for Heather Armstrong it turned out to be a savvy career move, as illustrated by her very popular blog.

Petite anglaise
petiteanglaise.com

"Gross misconduct" was the charge levelled at secretary Catherine Sanderson by her accountant employers; again, few outside the building would have been able to identify the company she worked for (her only clues were that a portrait of the Queen hung in the lobby and that they served Tetley tea to guests) but her vivid descriptions of her working day were clearly a little too vivid. Following her sacking, her readership went up from three thousand per day to over thirty thousand, and a six-figure book deal was signed. Not only that, she was eventually awarded a five-figure sum by an employment tribunal.

The Woolamaloo Gazette
woolamaloo.org.uk

Bookseller Joe Gordon had worked in his local Edinburgh bookstore for eleven years before he was fired for referring to his boss as "evil" in his anonymous blog. While the store claimed that he had cast shame on the company, Gordon saw it as little more than casual backchat – the kind of thing that you might discuss in the pub after work over a few pints. Ironically, Gordon's dismissal brought far more shame on the company than it would have done if they'd just had a quiet word in his ear. The story hit the news and traffic to Gordon's blog immediately shot up. He still sells books for a living, but is probably a little more cautious about lampooning his colleagues online.

Diary of a flight attendant

queenofsky.journalspace.com

Many are lured into becoming flight attendants with the promise of travel around the world, a racy lifestyle and, of course, the complimentary moist lemon scented cleansing squares. Ellen Simonetti, however, just told it exactly how it was – unembellished, irreverent details about the daily routine, and the tedium of drawing people's attention to their nearest emergency exit. While she never identified Delta Airlines as her employer, they found out pretty quickly when Simonetti posted a picture of herself, in uniform, on a Delta aeroplane. In her post-flight attendant career, she has written for several newspapers, published a book and been at the forefront of the debate surrounding bloggers' rights and freedom of speech.

Anger, revenge and humiliation

- - - - - - - - - - - - - - - -

There's nothing like unleashing your untrammelled anger on the Internet. It's brilliant. The relative anonymity of it all, coupled with the fleeting nature of online interaction, means that you can express strongly held opinions about anyone at all, call them a cretinous imbecile with the intelligence of shampoo and immediately disappear into the ether, satisfied that justice has been dispensed. There's no comeback; rarely will anyone come knocking at your door wielding a flick knife. And, let's

face it, it's easy to accuse someone of moronic stupidity if your username is something like "Spanglekitty" and they're "Barry The Wolf".

But the ease with which we can vent our spleens can make for a very vicious playground indeed. Opprobrium might suddenly be heaped upon us by dimwitted strangers who would never even bother looking up the word "opprobrium"; for them it's a case of act now, think later – and "U SUCK" usually represents the limit of their analytical powers. You might be a victim, an innocent party, but once the viral effect starts to snowball you're very unlikely to get a fair hearing.

On the other hand, if a wronged party is able to strike the first blow, the level playing field of the Internet allows them to get their revenge: we'll see companies such as Apple, Comcast, and AOL getting unwelcome publicity as the result of imaginative, home grown publicity campaigns, and fraudsters brought up short thanks to the valiant efforts of ongoing pranks such as the 419Eater.

Aside from one notable exception, we've steered clear of "flame wars", or forum based slanging matches; one famed Internet cartoon (tinyurl.com/2vovfg) summed these up nicely by depicting someone who refuses to be torn away from their computer and come to bed, and when asked why, replies: "Because someone is WRONG on the Internet." But hey, someone is always wrong on the Internet – and sometimes you've just got to take a deep breath and let it go.

So, while we've seen reluctant Internet stars in an earlier chapter, this next section represents the real underbelly of Internet fame. There's not a lot of celebration going on here; this lot have become notorious either for hating, or being hated – and in every one of these links, someone comes out looking not particularly great. And, in some cases, downright awful.

Worst CV ever
veoh.com/videos/e1336748NgyMqyG

Most of us would apply for a job enclosing a CV and a covering letter meekly outlining the ways in which we weren't totally inappropriate for the job. Yale student Aleksey Vayner, however, chose to direct and star in a ludicrous seven-minute film entitled *Impossible Is Nothing*, smugly detailing his philosophy of personal development alongside footage of him weightlifting, playing tennis and, most notably, ballroom dancing. One blog in particular (tinyurl.com/m7ldx) took considerable delight in lampooning the hapless Vayner, and linking to a spoof video entitled *Impossible Is The Opposite Of Possible*.

The 419 eater
419eater.com

Imagine that you were a wealthy individual who needed to transfer a huge sum of cash to a third party. The first thing you'd do would be to email several thousand strangers in a plea for help, right? Of course not. But over a thousand people each year fall victim to such scams, on average losing $20,000 each. It might seem pointless to fight this menace with surreal humour, but this website makes fraudsters think twice by engaging them in rambling correspondence and, in some cases, persuading them to send photographs of themselves in costume. Or, memorably, with a loaf of bread balanced on their head.

How not to parent
youtube.com/watch?v=VhO-OE931D4

Boys don't like receiving items of clothing for Christmas, because trousers don't beep, socks aren't operated by remote control and shirts don't have a liquid crystal display. And if the clothes are packed up in an Xbox 360 box, making you think that what you're actually unwrapping is a games console, well, that's got to hurt. Here's footage of such a moment: as the boy's face registers every emotion from delight through confusion, betrayal and ultimately despair, the family just laugh. The tongue lashing the parents received in the blogosphere was overwhelming. Don't watch this if you're feeling emotionally fragile.

Flame war follies

werewolves.org/~follies

Online forums can be vicious places. Arguments rage, people leave in a huff and then ten minutes later they're back, saying things they'd wish they'd said before storming out. And without the nuances of facial expression and tone of voice, a casual aside can imply that you want to have a fight in a local car park. This is the tale of the longest argument ever waged on the Internet, which pitted game designer David Smart and his allies against a whole army of people who thought his game, *Battlecruiser 3000AD*, was rubbish. Never was the phrase "leave it, it's not worth it" more appropriate.

spEak You're bRanes

tinyurl.com/yryysf

According to most news gathering organizations, our opinion matters. Some would have us believe that our views are worth as much as those of accredited experts. So we're urged to contribute our half-baked, ill considered analyses of everything from immigration to global warming, and as a result many news websites become overloaded with our cretinous, misspelled pronouncements. Unwilling to engage in these pointless debates, contributors to SYB retire to a safe distance and mercilessly savage their stupidity. And, unsurprisingly, the blog is hugely popular.

Considering its clean lines and appearance, spEak You're bRanes presents an extraordinary amalgamation of tangential mental outpourings.

Why can't I own a Canadian?
cronus.com/laura

It's not entirely clear who penned this sideswipe against right-wing US radio personality Laura Schlessinger back in May 2000 in response to her forthright restatement of the Bible's zero tolerance stance on homosexuality. Its popularity led to several people claiming credit, but whoever's responsible, it's a fantastic riposte. "Most of my male friends get their hair trimmed," it reads, "even though this is expressly forbidden by Lev.19:27. How should they die?" It eventually landed in the inbox of a writer on US drama series *The West Wing*; a scene based on the email cropped up in an episode later that year.

Call 911 for a cheeseburger
break.com/index/burger_king_911.html

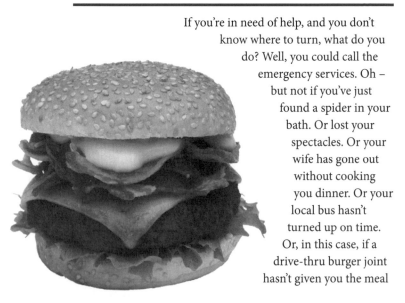

If you're in need of help, and you don't know where to turn, what do you do? Well, you could call the emergency services. Oh – but not if you've just found a spider in your bath. Or lost your spectacles. Or your wife has gone out without cooking you dinner. Or your local bus hasn't turned up on time. Or, in this case, if a drive-thru burger joint hasn't given you the meal you requested. What's particularly nice here is the withering sarcasm dished out by the operator in response. "You're supposed to be protecting me!" cries the woman. "What are we protecting you from?" comes the reply. "A wrong cheeseburger?"

Roommate from hell
tinyurl.com/4dvbj

Stories of disastrous house sharing experiences have become common currency online, but this particular tale is so astonishing, so graphic in its detail and unrelenting in its horror, that it puts disagreements over the ownership of a jar of peanut butter into stark perspective. The original site that hosted the tale had to remove it because of sheer weight of traffic, but this kind soul has conserved it for future generations to marvel at. If you can't believe that someone would ever have to construct a complex entry system to their room using a remote control car for fear of his clothes being defecated on, just read this.

Bus Uncle
youtube.com/watch?v=EsYRQkmVifg

Bus Uncle was the innocuous name given to a Hong Kong resident after mobile phone footage of him screaming at a fellow passenger on a night bus began to sweep across the Far East, and eventually – thanks to a subtitled version – the world. It was merely a gentle tap on the shoulder and a request that he might lower his voice that incurred Bus Uncle's wrath. After threatening violence and his intent to fornicate with the shocked youth's mother, he continued to yell: "I have pressure! You have pressure!" – indicating that he'd been skipping important anger management classes.

The taser

The phrase "Don't tase me, bro!" had the dubious accolade of reaching number one in *Time Magazine*'s "T-shirt Worthy Slogans" in 2007 – and its ubiquity was mainly thanks to the Internet. A taser, for those of you unfamiliar with modern law-enforcement, is an electroshock weapon used by police – particularly in North America – to bring unruly and uncooperative people under control; its deployment generally causes those on the receiving end to scream in agony, writhe around the floor in pain and quickly shed their previous belligerence.

The weapons have been mired in controversy; while they are only intended to stun, Amnesty International has documented 245 deaths that have occurred after tasers have been used. So you could put the enormous popularity of taser videos down to our collective concern at the overuse of such weapons, and a need for us to see with our own eyes the evidence of police brutality. On the other hand, it could be because some people get some sadistic delight from seeing human beings having fifty thousand volts pushed through them by a hi-tech cattle prod.

Incidents only reach prominence, of course, when someone nearby happens to be filming on their mobile phone. The one which caused "don't tase me, bro!" to be emblazoned across American chests may, in fact, have been the result of a prank gone wrong: a student at Florida university by the name of Andrew Meyer asked a stranger to film him just before he put a question to former presidential candidate John Kerry at a student forum, and it's thought that he did intend to cause some low-key havoc. However, he probably wasn't expecting things to kick off quite in the way that they did: when his microphone was cut mid-question, his protests were met with several taser blasts from a police officer (*youtube.com/watch?v=6bVa6jn4rpE*). By contrast, another student – this time from UCLA – was doing nothing more than quietly reading in a library when his refusal to produce his university ID (*youtube.com/watch?v=AyvrqcxNlFs*) resulted in a taser being deployed. The student claimed that he was being racially targeted; the incident was followed by widespread protests, lawsuits, international condemnation and millions of views on the Internet.

These clips can make for grim viewing; it's hard to justify the use of tasers on either this female protestor in Pittsburgh (*youtube. com/watch?v=kA8fD6YvyJk*) or this motorist in Utah (*youtube. com/watch?v=lMaMYL_shxc*). But there are also clips which show people willingly being subjected to the might of the taser, including these three burly policemen bobbing about in agony on a bench (*youtube.com/ watch?v=qzbP9x9chc0*); and, presumably in return for cash, some B-list celebs. When a group of them – including Jack Osbourne and Latoya Jackson – participated in a reality show called, would you believe, *Armed And Famous*, they were required by Indiana state law to undergo a taser shock before being allowed to carry one on the streets (*youtube.com/ watch?v=by5_8SpGX-E*). One celebrity complains afterwards of having "an enlarged testicle"; bearing in mind Amnesty's figures, he might consider himself lucky.

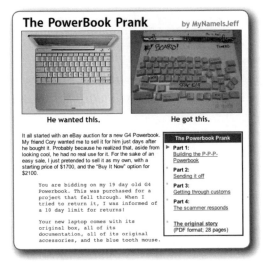

The PowerBook Prank — by MyNameIsJeff

He wanted this.

He got this.

It all started with an eBay auction for a new G4 Powerbook. My friend Cory wanted me to sell it for him just days after he bought it. Probably because he realized that, aside from looking cool, he had no real use for it. For the sale of an easy sale, I just pretended to sell it as my own, with a starting price of $1700, and the "Buy It Now" option for $2100.

You are bidding on my 19 day old G4 Powerbook. This was purchased for a project that fell through. When I tried to return it, I was informed of a 10 day limit for returns!

Your new laptop comes with its original box, all of its original documentation, all of its original accessories, and the blue tooth mouse.

The Powerbook Prank

▶ **Part 1:**
Building the P-P-P-Powerbook

Part 2:
Sending it off

Part 3:
Getting through customs

Part 4:
The scammer responds

The original story
(PDF format; 28 pages)

Fake laptop
zug.com/pranks/powerbook

Any time you make an online purchase, there's always a niggle in the back of your mind as to whether the item will actually turn up. But sellers have to contend with dishonesty, too – particularly with "escrow" scams, where the promised funds just never materialize. If you're clued up, however, they're easy to spot – and a chap called Jeff fought fire with fire when his fake overseas buyer "bought" a laptop from him; he sent one made out of a ring binder, a broken keyboard and some glitter, and declared its customs value as $2100 – stiffing the recipient for massive import taxes.

eBay revenge
amirtofangsazan.blogspot.com

If a shop fails to replace faulty goods they're likely to face legal action. But those who sell knackered second-hand goods online can face a far more inventive barrage of retaliatory action. When a student bought a faulty laptop on eBay and his requests for a refund fell on deaf ears, he extracted the embarrassing contents of the hard drive – including ninety pictures of women's legs that had been snapped on public transport – and posted them on a blog that quickly received over a million hits. Over a year later, no money has been refunded, and the vendor continues to be named and shamed.

Tom Cruise, guardian angel
tinyurl.com/yre7c6

While Tom Cruise's religious beliefs won't be news to anyone, this video is a perfect example of the futility of trying to suppress anything online. If you object strongly to something being made public – as the Church of Scientology did when this clip featuring Cruise talking about his faith was leaked – and succeed in getting it removed, it'll only pop up somewhere else an hour later. "Being a Scientologist, when you drive past an accident," said Cruise, "you know you have to do something about it because you know you're the only one that can really help." That's Tom, along with a team of paramedics, presumably.

Lee Hotti
tinyurl.com/2d3btt

Many people have regretted uploading personal details and pictures to the Internet, but few errors of judgement have been exploited so enthusiastically as a messageboard posting by one "Lee Hotti" of a picture of himself and some almost identical friends at a party in New Jersey. The original thread received over two million hits and has since been deleted – as has the tribute site at leehotti.com which contained defaced versions of the picture – but this video memorial remains. Hotti was unrepentant. "If you wanna start somethign," he typed, evidently in a hurry, "u better be ready to deal with us."

21st at the Ritz
tinyurl.com/2fxnfx

Lucy Gao, an intern with Citigroup, had big plans for her 21st birthday party, and was keen to leave absolutely nothing to chance. But her meticulous plans – detailed in an email and subsequently forwarded to inboxes across the world – would put arrangements for a royal visit to shame. Her friends were assigned precise times of arrival at London's Ritz Hotel, staggered over fifteen-minute intervals; they were given exact words to announce to the concierge; and were informed that "the more upper class you dress, the less likely you shall be denied entry." It's not known whether any of said friends bothered turning up.

Pranks and practical jokes

While many of the links in this chapter are driven by an undercurrent of anger or contempt, there's also revenge of a milder kind. You could call it "harmless fun", or even "entertainment". No one was harmed in the creation of these links. Embarrassed, perhaps. Scared, occasionally. But the important thing is that no lawsuits are pending. As far as we know.

Tom Mabe is no longer with us
howtoprankatelemarketer.ytmnd.com

Spare a thought for the hapless call centre worker. They're being paid a minimal, if not minumum, wage to call people who don't want to speak to them; for hour after hour they have to put up with a grim cycle of introduction, interruption and rejection. To make matters worse, they care even less about the subject matter of the call than its recipient. And then, if they're really unlucky, they might call an American humorist at the peak of his improvisatory powers, who accuses them of being involved in a murder plot. Originally broadcast on radio, the clip gained massive notoriety via the Net.

We suck

harvardsucks.org

Back in 1961, students from Caltech, a college in Pasadena, pulled off an incredible stunt at an American football game at the Pasadena Rose Bowl. Thanks to meticulous planning, they succeeded in getting supporters of the Washington Huskies to hold cards aloft to spell CALTECH, rather than the expected HUSKIES. Particularly surreal, because Caltech weren't even participating in the game. In this 2004 reenactment, students from Yale conned Harvard students into proudly proclaiming WE SUCK; the cash that they made flogging posters of the prank online was donated to a tsunami relief fund.

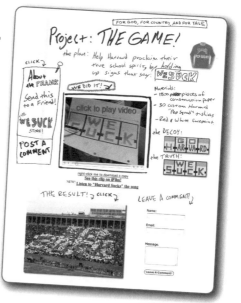

Students playing practical jokes? Whatever next? Yale get one over on their Harvard rivals thanks to an ingenious bit of card-switching under the stadium seats.

Maze of concentration
winterrowd.com/maze

Okay, so, I turn the volume up on the computer… Right. Now, by using the mouse, I manoeuvre the dot through the maze, yeah? Okay… well, this isn't particularly difficult… Level 2, okay, well, it's a little trickier now… er no, sorry – could you

answer the phone for me? I'm just playing this maze game, thanks… Level 3… Ouch. This is really hard, now. If I can just g– aaaaagggggggghhh!! Arrrghhh!! So many people have been scared out of their wits by this unassuming game, that videos of people's reactions to the grisly denouement have become viral hits in themselves (youtube.com/watch?v=oh87njiWTmw).

Rick rolling
youtube.com/watch?v=oHg5SJYRHA0

It's one of the most pervasive online practical jokes; it's also one of the easiest to perpetrate, and probably one of the most unamusing. I could play the joke on you right here by just urging you to go to the above link – but you deserve better, so I'll tell you: all it is is the video to "Never Gonna Give You Up" by Rick Astley. That's all. Nothing more, nothing less. The poor souls who end up being directed there – usually in the hope of seeing lurid pornography – are said to have been Rickrolled; it's the only possible explanation for the various instances of this video having pulled in over ten million unlucky viewers. For an earlier and possibly more amusing example of the genre, see tinyurl.com/6cj3f.

Ride home from the bachelor party

youtube.com/watch?v=a3NxGDZKP2s

A gentle doze in the back of a people carrier, sleeping off the excesses of the night before, comes to a brutal end when the snoozer's travelling companions unleash a collective, shrill, blood-curdling scream – presumably at some imminent freeway catastrophe. He responds as any of us would: snapping wide awake, joining in the yelling and looking utterly terrified. Of course, there was no catastrophe. They were only having him on. But as a result his blood pressure went through the roof, and in the ensuing melee he squashed the sandwich he was planning to have for lunch. Poor chap.

Men are pigs

Holla back, New York

hollabacknyc.blogspot.com

By snapping and posting pictures of men who attempt to sexually harass women in and around New York, Holla Back aims to shame the perpetrators and show other women what they look like. While some men probably feel a misplaced sense of pride at achieving global recognition of their ability to say "hey, nice tits", snaps of this kind have actually resulted in arrests. Similar sites have sprung up across the US, and while some accuse its users of being cybervigilantes, you have to applaud anything that dissuades men from covertly masturbating on public transport.

You ate the food
tinyurl.com/htz5w

Internet dating can be a lottery. People describe themselves as "fun loving", but when you meet them they'll immediately start to sob and recount how they were bullied at school. They might state that they are of "average build", knowing that they regularly get wedged in ticket barriers. When Joanne accepted a dinner date with Darren – who considers himself "cute, tall and funny" – she didn't expect to receive an email afterwards demanding $50 for her half of the meal. Followed by voicemails threatening legal action. "You ate the food," said Darren. "Do the right thing." Joanne did the right thing. She ignored him.

Never date him
neverdatehim.com

The emotion generated by being dumped or cheated on is a powerful thing; it can make us jettison piles of clothes out of bedroom windows, burn stacks of letters and generate masses of self-indulgent poetry. This site became notable for its raw recountings of dating mishaps ("this man is a liar, a cheat and a meth addict"), while revealing the sites the offenders hang out on, along with their usernames. (I'd be suspicious of someone calling themselves "cockwand69", wouldn't you?) See also neverdateher.com, horriblebreakup.com and divorceventing.com. And then attempt to calm down with a nice cup of tea.

Ketchupgate
tinyurl.com/canat

Sackings due to accidental sending and rampant forwarding of inappropriate emails are regular news. Many of them consist of indiscreet descriptions of boozing and shagging, proudly suffixed with the company name; being associated with prostitutes, oral sex and hard drinking just isn't good for business, you know. But in this case, the offence was one of sheer stinginess: a high earning employee demanded £4 from his secretary towards a dry-cleaning bill after she'd got ketchup on his trousers. No one knows exactly how the ketchup got there, but the publicity received by her frosty reply ended up losing him his job.

Revenge of the little guy

Dance, monkeyboy!
tinyurl.com/ydkftz

"I love this company," yells Microsoft CEO Steve Ballmer as he leaps and whirls around the stage at a Microsoft employee convention. "Whooooo!" he shrieks, gasping for breath. "Aaaaaaaaa!" Odd. But then again, if you had a net worth of $15bn, you'd probably be given to similarly unhinged public displays of affection towards the company that made your fortune. Ballmer, however, probably doesn't give a

Steve Ballmer seems absolutely convinced of the merits of Windows Vista.

hoot about the fact that this video made him the laughing stock of the Internet, thanks to feverish link forwarding by anyone who has had the slightest beef about Microsoft. Which is, let's face it, everybody.

iPod's dirty secret

neistat.com/movies/ipodsdirtysecret

Back in 2003, Casey Neistat's iPod battery died after just eighteen months of use. He called Apple, and was advised that to replace the battery would cost $255 plus postage and packing, and that at that price he "might as well go get a new one". Neistat responded by stencilling iPod posters in his neighbourhood with the phrase "iPod's unreplaceable battery only lasts 18 months", and the video of him doing so was subsequently downloaded over a million times. He didn't get arrested for vandalism, but Apple did change their iPod battery policy. Coincidence? (Well, apparently it was a coincidence, but let's not spoil the story.)

You might not condone vandalism, but how else can you make a multinational take notice of your complaint? Watch Casey Neistat's video and let your conscience battle it out.

Sleeping on the job
youtube.com/watch?v=CvVp7b5gzqU

In this updated version of the Goldilocks fairy tale, the answer to the question "Who's been sleeping on MY couch?" is answered pretty easily: it's a cable technician for US company Comcast, let into the house to repair a faulty modem. It's debatable whether filming the guy and sharing the video online was a nicer gesture than gently shaking him awake, but it certainly created more of a stir. Incredibly, this is not the only time this has happened – another Comcast technician (youtube.com/watch?v=6kQRFB-8cEs) ended up on *Fox News* as a result of slumbering during working hours.

Cancel the account
insignificantthoughts.com/2006/06/13/cancelling-aol

In any relationship, when one of you decides it's over, there's not a great deal that the jilted party can do about it. But when Vincent Ferrari delivered the bad news over the telephone to his Internet provider, AOL, the jilted multinational refused to accept that it would no longer be able to bill his credit card for $14.95 every month. The AOL representative – later fired by the company – took the decision personally, coming up with all kinds of reasons to keep the relationship alive, and eventually asked the thirty-year-old Ferrari to put his father on the phone instead. Ferrari was unwavering. They're no longer an item.

I hate my cable company
ihaterogers.ca

Internet service providers have a tough time of it. Rarely does anyone speak up to say how fantastically speedy their broadband connection is, or what good value their monthly package represents. But no one throws themselves so wholeheartedly into their hatred of a communications provider as much as Adam Sherman, whose extensive, pithy and popular website is devoted to badmouthing his local Toronto-based cable company. Anyone who sends in particularly high quality horror stories can even win a "highly coveted, incredibly mediocre and unusually rare" I Hate Rogers t-shirt.

Conspiracies, hoaxes and spoofs

The Web has facilitated a non-stop dialogue between those who create sites and those that read them, and so it's the easiest thing in the world to accuse something or somebody of being a fake. It's a kneejerk, single word response that you see in the comments sections of all kinds of Web content, from videos of manual dexterity ("Fake!") to first person accounts of alien abduction ("Fake!"), from previously unseen photos of terrorist atrocities ("Fake!") to claims of astounding success on a gambling site ("Fake!"). There's very little you can do when someone shouts "Fake!" at you, rather than say "No, it's true, really" – but by that time your detractor will

have long since disappeared into the ether, taking his or her staunchly held beliefs with them.

Of course, certain levels of both cynicism and trust are very healthy – but the Internet breeds both like rabbits on fertility drugs. While one group of people is slamming a website for being economical with the truth, those same people will be happy to give credence to all manner of other claims on alternative sites that just happen to back up their various hunches. You see this most acutely in sites devoted to 9/11, the assassination of JFK and the moon landings; it seems that the rationale we use for believing a piece of information online has become horribly skewed because, somehow, we perceive all kinds of dubious sources as having the same weight. Anyone who sticks anything up on a webpage (particularly if it's well designed) suddenly acquires authority – becomes an expert, even – so getting to the bottom of the mystery in hand can be incredibly difficult.

And then, of course, there are the pranksters who play on our gullibility by setting up hoax websites such as the well-known Online Pregnancy Test. But while they go to great lengths to make their sites as absurd as possible, there are always people for whom nothing is "Fake!". If everyone had a healthy dose of common sense, most of the links below would never have become viral sensations. But while we know, deep down, that we shouldn't believe everything we read on the Internet, we often do – and often it's the most unlikely sites that seem to sneak under our radar.

Is it? Or isn't it?

Catching glasses on your face
youtube.com/watch?v=-prfAENSh2k

Flipping a cigarette from a pack and catching it in your mouth has finally been superseded as the epitome of cool: the new trick is to catch a pair of shades that have been flung casually across the room squarely on the bridge of your nose. How we'd love to believe that this video is kosher, and that it's a trick that we could accomplish with a few hours of practice during which we'd only occasionally be stabbed in the left eye with one of the arms. Sadly, it's a very neatly executed trick involving reversed camera footage and, well, a piece of string. See the full explanation at tinyurl.com/36zj5s.

These days, it's not enough to casually sport a pair of sunglasses to adopt an air of laid-back sophistication. Now, as this clip shows, you've got to get a friend to lob them onto your face from twenty metres away.

Psycho ex-girlfriend
scherle.com/psychoexgirlfriend/voicemails.html

Rambling answerphone messages from hysterical ex-partners are prime candidates for being immediately deleted, even before you've reached the bit that says "to replay this message press 1", but Mark McElwain rewound, replayed, recorded and immortalized 53 of them on a hugely popular website. Voices of suspicion were raised, however, when attempts to track down the jilted woman failed; the website disappeared not long afterwards and, seven years on, no one really knows whether it was real, or just an elaborate way of letting the world know that ladies just can't get enough of Mark McElwain.

Hot tub accident

break.com/index/embarrasing_hot_tub_accident.html

Some virals can't help but furrow brows and trigger extended debates. This clip of a woman having what you might term an "accident" in a jacuzzi is too slick and too nicely set up to possibly be real. But on the other hand, why would anyone spend time and money setting up a scene of someone defacating in a whirlpool bath? Are they trying to sell us something, perhaps? But what, for goodness sake? Anti-diarrhoea tablets? Surely not jacuzzis? Home insurance? Is it a film trailer? Or what?

The Asian Prince
geocities.com/asianprince_213

There are good ways of ensnaring your ideal partner – washing occasionally, refraining from too much violence, remembering not to sob uncontrollably in their presence – and there are bad ways, for example putting up a large airbrushed picture of yourself on the Internet along with blurb that would make even the most desperate woman flee. "As well as being an excellent lover," says the Asian Prince, "I am also excellent with cars. Here is a picture of my Honda Civic." While the pictured lothario certainly does exist – Vietnamese popstar Tuan Anh – the website was the work of someone who was just a bit bored one afternoon.

Claire Swire
claireswireonline.tripod.com

An email forwarded as rampantly as the one supposedly tapped out by Claire Swire is bound to raise not only eyebrows, but also suspicions as to its veracity. Her boyfriend, Bradley Chait, proudly forwarded the two-line comment she sent to him complimenting the palatability of his bodily fluids, but the idea that it might "go no further" was laughable: within the week, pretty much everyone with a computer knew about it. Chait, in the immediate aftermath, claimed it was a hoax, but there are enough clues knocking around to indicate otherwise, without having to get intimate with Mr Chait to secure the ultimate proof.

The big questions

Search on Google for the phrase "I'm really sorry, you were right all along", and you'll find that it returns a grand total of zero hits. It's not a phrase you hear very often online; well rehearsed rhetoric is spouted, repeated and spread, and opinions become entrenched as people whip each other up into a truth-seeking frenzy. The common thread that runs through the following links is the idea that We Are Being Lied To. And while most would concede that this is undoubtedly true from time to time, most of us don't buy the whole kit 'n' kaboodle. Yes, sometimes politicians are, in the words of Alan Clark, "economical with the actualité" – but that doesn't mean they're necessarily dedicated to murdering voters in the search for votes.

Hidden reptilian agenda
reptilianagenda.com

Conduct a quick poll among your friends, and check how many of them have ever been abducted by a shape-shifting reptilian humanoid. Three? Four? What, none? Hm. Well, judging by the wealth of evidence on this website, all of us should be on our guard. There are tales of a blonde jazz singer who engaged in sexual acts with these reptiles ("Why would I make it up?" she says, "it doesn't exactly help my singing career, does it?" Answer: Yes) along with other burning questions, such as "How much did Jim Morrison know?" (Answer: The lyrics to "Light My Fire"?) and "Are faeries abducting humans?" (Answer: No.)

JFK: secret service standdown

youtube.com/watch?v=XY02Qkuc_f8

Twenty-five years after JFK's death, the debate surrounding its circumstances shows not the remotest signs of dying down. Precious hours of people's lives are spent wringing the last drops of conjecture from the most scrutinized evidence in the history of mankind – and it's not as if any of them are working towards a new theory that will take the world by storm; they're just participants in a massive, unmoderated, free-for-all squabble. Who knows what comments will appear under this video by the time you read this, but one thing they're unlikely to say is "Well, it doesn't really matter, does it, he's dead."

This clip, that allegedly shows secret service agent Henry Rybka being ordered to stand down from his position at the rear of JFK's limousine, has been seized upon as another indication that things were not quite as they seemed on November 22, 1963.

Secrets in Bohemian Grove

video.google.ca/videoplay?docid=-
82095917705734983

There's little doubt that a number of powerful figures in the world of politics do indeed descend on woodland north of San Francisco every year, hang out for a few days and take part in

Snopes.com

Snopes, named after an irksome family in the novels of William Faulkner, is a renowned myth-busting, rumour-scotching website that's the first place to go when you want tall tales denied or, more rarely, confirmed. The layout might be ham-fisted, decidedly 2001 and long overdue a rehaul, but the information therein is extensive, meticulously researched, and entertainingly written to boot. Was Houdini really killed by an unexpected punch to the stomach? It would seem not. Is Michael Jackson's phone number contained within the barcode of the album *Thriller*? Of course it isn't – but that hasn't stopped hundreds of people dialling it on the offchance; if they'd gone to Snopes first, they could have saved themselves a few cents and a few seconds of embarrassment.

The site was founded by Barbara Hamel and David Mikkelson, who first met online in a discussion forum dedicated to urban myths and folklore. Their shared interest in debunking stories of questionable origin led them not only to launch Snopes, but also get married – although it's unclear which came first. But you can bet that if there were ever any raging online debate over this fact, Snopes would be there to clear the matter up.

The strength of the site is that it's level-headed, completely unhysterical and considers each story purely on the evidence strange rituals. After all, outspoken conspiracy theorist Alex Jones gained entry to the event and documented it for posterity. The question is whether burning a human effigy in front of a forty-foot owl is merely continuing a fine, upstanding tradition and is a perfectly harmless way to spend an evening, or whether it masks sinister, Satanic practices. (No guesses as to which side of the fence Alex Jones is on.)

available. And so it's certainly not hellbent on dismissing every possible rumour that circulates – although, in the Internet age, more will be baloney than not; it just provides a simple colour coding of true, false or undetermined, along with references to information sources. With online discussion generally consisting of endless, tedious speculation, Snopes comes as a welcome relief, because you know you'll be told it straight. Having said that, it's inevitable that some people will speculate that Barbara and David are part of some evil New World Order. But hey, that's the Internet for you.

Are thieves in shopping malls using perfume bottles to render their victims unconscious? No. Does taping a penny to a bee sting help it heal? Possibly. Are green potatoes poisonous? Yes! How do we know? Because Snopes.com says so – click through from the rows of category icons to uncover the truth.

Moon landing hoax
apfn.org/apfn/moon.htm

So, did the Apollo 11 mission consist of a spectacular blast off from The Kennedy Space Center, a 385,000km journey to the moon, a couple of hours spent on its dusty surface and a return home to universal acclaim, wonder and admiration?

Terrorist conspiracies

If you can think of a terrorist atrocity for which there's a unanimously agreed explanation – who did it, where it was done and why they did it – you've probably not turned on your computer lately. The cataclysmic events that unfolded in the US in 2001, Spain in 2004 and the UK in 2005 might seem to be fairly straightforward, but while judges and investigators pored over the evidence and came up with an official version of events, online debate gave rise to all kinds of alternative scenarios – and all of a sudden, everyone was an expert. You don't have to have a balanced, rational argument to be heard loud and clear; you just have to have an argument. And so we can see "proof" that the World Trade Center was destroyed by a controlled explosion (*youtube.*

"Sheeple" is the name that conspiracy theorists give to those who dare to dismiss their propositions – such as those found of the meticulously presented Rense.com.

Rense.com

UAL Flight 93 Landed Safely At Cleveland Hopkins Airport
Plane Lands In Cleveland - Bomb Feared Aboard
8-7-4

Reported by 9News Staff
Web produced by Liz Foreman
9/11/01 11:43:57 AM

A Boeing 767 out of Boston made an emergency landing Tuesday at Cleveland Hopkins International Airport due to concerns that it may have a bomb aboard, said Mayor Michael R. White.

White said the plane had been moved to a secure area of the airport, and was evacuated.

United identified the plane as Flight 93. The airline did not say how many people were aboard the flight.

United said it was also "deeply concerned" about another flight, Flight 175, a Boeing 767, which was bound from Boston to Los Angeles.

On behalf of the airline CEO James Goodwin said: "The thoughts of everyone at United are with the passengers and crew of these flights. Our prayers are also with everyone on the ground who may have been involved.

"United is working with all the relevant authorities, including the FBI, to obtain further information on these flights," he said.

Or did NASA just pack Aldrin and Armstrong off to a film set with Stanley Kubrick, suspend them from a series of wires and release the resulting footage to television stations? While the latter option would have been better for NASA's budget and required far less organisation, the conspiracy theories are quickly dismantled by this site: redzero.demon.co.uk/moonhoax.

com/watch?v=w-0Ms7mId34), that Flight 93 didn't crash into a field and actually landed safely at Cleveland Airport (rense.com/general56/flfight.htm), and that a missile rather than a plane hit the Pentagon (pentagonstrike.co.uk/sott/ATS_article.php).

You might also be persuaded that the Madrid bombings were orchestrated by the country's opposition party in order to get into power, and that the London explosions were actually caused by a power surge, with actors hired to play survivors and a demolition company brought in to make the whole thing look convincing. And throughout all of this, you'll repeatedly see the word "truth", deployed endlessly in a range of eye-catching fonts. While conspiracy sites are hugely popular, it's difficult to know how many people take the claims seriously, and how many are just visiting to see what the loons are saying today. But just to be on the safe side, those committed to debunking conspiracy theories have been hard at work fighting the "troofers". You can see the widely viewed conspiracy film Loose Change (loosechange911.com) rebutted point by point in Screw Loose Change (screwloosechange.blogspot.com), and Penn & Teller give their own expletive-filled reaction on YouTube (youtube.com/watch?v=kcrF346sS_I) – but remember, if you decide that it's the government accounts that you believe, that either makes you a confused, blinkered idiot or, worse, part of the conspiracy. In short, you can't win.

Dear everyone in my address book

Email forwarding was to the early part of this decade what Web 2.0 is to the latter; both gave us all an unmissable chance to spread rumours as fast as possible, without stopping to put our brains into gear first.

Make money fast
tinyurl.com/2uzhgs

It's the Internet version of those chain letter scams and pyramid schemes that offer riches beyond your wildest dreams in return for being a bit gullible. A surprising number of people, it seems, are happy to send off money in brown envelopes unquestioningly, and a chap called Dave Rhodes – if indeed he exists at all – used this email to dangle the possibility of making $50,000 in sixty days in return for sending out $5 in cash to complete strangers. Needless to say, this unmissable one million percent investment opportunity doesn't work; all that happens in sixty days is that you lose $5 worth of self-esteem.

Neiman-Marcus cookie
tinyurl.com/3yfppa

After enjoying some cookies in the cafeteria of her local Neiman-Marcus department store, a woman asked the waitress for the recipe and was told it would cost "two fifty". After discovering that she'd been billed $250 instead of $2.50, she took revenge by emailing the recipe to all her friends, urging them to spread it far and wide and "stick it to the man". Thing is, Neiman-Marcus never had a cookie recipe (although they've developed one since – savvy marketing!) and the $250 cookie recipe is merely a cookie recipe. Although it has become the most famous cookie recipe in the world as a result – no mean feat.

Good times
cityscope.net/hoax1

Any email you receive warning you about a computer virus is in itself viral, and almost certainly a hoax. Playing on our naivety in the early days of the Internet, the "Good Times" email warned of how our computers would imminently enter an nth-complexity infinite binary loop. Which doesn't exist. Parodies, inevitably, followed: "Good Times will give you Dutch Elm disease. It will leave the toilet seat up. It will make a batch of methamphetamine in your bathtub and then leave bacon cooking on the stove while it goes out to chase grade schoolers with your new snowblower."

Spoofs

The fake Steve Jobs
fakesteve.blogspot.com

The name of this blog immediately dispelled any idea that it might be real, but it took months to unmask the hoaxer who brilliantly lampooned the egotistical reputation of Apple boss Steve Jobs. It wasn't until a book manuscript started circulating that it was revealed to be journalist Dan Lyons – not an Apple insider, as was thought, but someone who actually had to go out and buy books and biographies to do research. "My plan at this

Preposterous eBay auctions

Hoax items are put up for sale on eBay all the time; hoax bidders then join in the fun, turning it into one huge, imaginary auction that eBay shuts down as quickly as they can – which, in turn, generates substantial column inches in the media. The online casino Golden Palace is certainly wise to this, regularly getting its name in the press for the outrageous sums it spends on fairly innocuous items: $650,000 for the right to name a recently discovered species of monkey; $15,199 to change a vendor's name to goldenpalace.com; $10,000 for another vendor to permanently tattoo the casino's name on her forehead, and $28,000 for a toasted cheese sandwich – with one bite taken from it – that was said to contain the image of the Virgin Mary.

Golden Palace paid up and, as far as we know, got what it wanted in return, but others weren't so lucky. The Australian man who tried to sell New Zealand was doing pretty well with a bid of $3000AUD before eBay pointed out that it wasn't his to sell; the German Language Association never got its €10 million when it tried to sell its mother tongue, and the student who attempted to sell his soul is still in possession of it some seven years later. But some that you'd be sure were hoaxes were, in fact, perfectly real: a Lotus Esprit sports car went for just 50p, while the Pope's old Volkswagen Gold went for an equally astonishing €188,938.88; the aircraft carrier HMS *Vengeance* was genuinely listed in 2004, but had to be removed when it was pointed out that weapons aren't allowed on eBay; a dribble of water in a plastic cup once touched by Elvis Presley fetched $455, while a leftover Brussels Sprout from a Christmas dinner went for an unlikely £99.50 – with the proceeds donated to charity, of course.

time is to live forever and to remain in charge here," wrote Fake Steve back in July 2007, "though perhaps with fewer restrictions on my power. The truth is, I am not human – I am a man-god, son of Zeus."

Aluminum foil deflector beanie
zapatopi.net/afdb

The wearing of tinfoil hats by schizophrenics anxious not to allow governments or aliens to read their thoughts hasn't done conspiracy theorists any favours; if they exhibit even the slightest tendency towards paranoia during Internet debates, they'll immediately be accused of wearing one. Lyle Zapato brought the hat up to date with this spoof website, which in turn spawned a book. Gloriously, he refused to step out of character in media interviews to promote the book (and indeed the hat) restating solemnly how rejuvenating it is to have rays repelled from your brain.

Say goodbye to those annoying bouts of having your mind controlled by extra-terrestrial forces with the all-new aluminium foil hat, as modelled on the above webpage.

Pets? Or food?
petsorfood.com

You'd have thought, wouldn't you, that a site set up to sell unwanted pets as food – ready-to-eat hamsters, Doberman steaks and exotic Komodo dragons – would be identified

BOILERPLATE

MECHANICAL MARVEL OF THE NINETEENTH CENTURY

Boilerplate was a mechanical man developed by **Professor Archibald Campion** during the 1880s and unveiled at the **1893 World's Columbian Exposition**.

Built in a small **Chicago laboratory**, Boilerplate was originally designed as a prototype soldier for use in resolving the conflicts of nations. Although it was the only such prototype, Boilerplate was eventually able to exercise its proposed function by participating in several **combat actions**.

In the mid-1890s, Boilerplate embarked on a series of expeditions to demonstrate its abilities, the most ambitious being **a voyage to Antarctica**. Boilerplate is one of history's great ironies, a technological milestone that remains largely unknown. Even in an age that gave birth to the automobile and aeroplane, a functioning mechanical man should have been accorded more significance.

*Boilerplate with **Archibald Campion**.*
Click to enlarge photo.

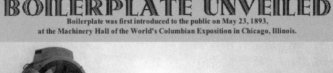

BOILERPLATE UNVEILED

Boilerplate was first introduced to the public on May 23, 1893,
at the Machinery Hall of the World's Columbian Exposition in Chicago, Illinois.

instantaneously as a fake. Which of course it is – but that didn't stop debate raging as to its veracity among the wide-eyed and pea-brained over at that hotbed of radical thought, Yahoo! Answers (tinyurl.com/2mglf3). "Is there a way that we can delete the website? That would be a good idea," says one upset animal lover. "I emailed them about it, and apparently it is REAL!" A voice of sanity then points out that they sell dodos. Which are extinct.

History of a Victorian-era robot

bigredhair.com/boilerplate

The discovery of evidence relating to Boilerplate, a prototypical robot built in the late nineteenth century from sheets of iron, pistons and grease, would have been an important moment for historians everywhere had it not been dreamt up by artist Paul Guinan. Again, the facts relating to Boilerplate's pivotal role in the Mexican Revolution should have ensured that no one was taken in; but apparently Guinan receives emails from students asking about Boilerplate's means of propulsion, and the robot even appeared in a novel, *The Shroud of the Thwacker*, after some less than diligent research.

The Ova Prima Foundation

ovaprima.org

It was well over two thousand years ago when first Aristotle, and then Plutarch, pondered over the tricky problem of whether the chicken or the egg came first. Neither of them could come up with a definitive answer, and so violent altercations and boozy brawls have ensued for the next couple of millennia as we wrestled with the issue. The Ova Prima Foundation – fake, of course – is dedicated to proving that it was the humble egg that begat the first chicken. Stephen Hawking reckons it's the egg, so they must be doing something right. If your kids ask you to explain why, just print off this impenetrable essay for them to digest (tinyurl.com/2uuu2h).

Free online pregnancy test
thepregnancytester.com

The Net has revolutionized communication, allowed us to buy goods and services from the supposed comfort of our own home, and has put a dizzying array of pornography at our fingertips – so surely it can help us find out if we're pregnant? Common sense should tell us that the medical scanning abilities of our computer monitor are severely limited but, as this site appears towards the top of Google's search results for "pregnancy test", it's bound to have taken a few people in. Note the very light grey writing that says "It's a joke, OK" – and get yourself down the chemist.

Create your own genetically healthy child
genochoice.com

Genochoice doesn't even own up to being a joke, preferring instead to tease out any secretly held sub-Nazi views on eugenics from the site's visitors, and allow them to believe for a fleeting moment that it would be possible to mail off a cheque to ensure that their son wouldn't be blighted in later life by male pattern baldness. I mean, which right-thinking parents wouldn't be willing to cough up $5,875 to "cure" their as yet unborn child from its 98 percent predisposition to homosexuality? Artist Virgil Wong did a brilliant job here in pastiching future medical technology.

Dog island
thedogisland.com

It's conceivable that dogs, if they were asked and able to give a coherent answer, would dearly love to break free from the tyranny of human oppression, put an end to tedious evening walks through bleak urban landscapes, give up the unimaginatively presented and overwhelmingly brown food and banish the mindless routines of chasing and fetching that seem to delight their owners so much. Well, there's something you can do for your dog; box him up and ship him off to Dog Island, a canine paradise set up just off the coast of Florida that's redefining the phrase "a dog's life", or would be, if it were true.

Landover Baptist
landoverbaptist.org

It's not that difficult to satirize the views of far right Christian fundamentalists such as Fred Phelps (of "God Hates Fags" fame) but to keep it up for as long as Chris Harper has, creating the ludicrous persona of Pastor Deacon Fred Smith and regularly delivering mock sermons on YouTube, shows true dedication to the atheist cause. Harper succeeds in provoking fury across the board, from left-wingers who don't get the joke and berate him for his extreme views, to right-wingers who realize that they're being savagely mocked; but the million visitors a month that the site receives surely proves that it's working for some people.

The Onion
theonion.com

The Onion has spawned many imitators, but remains the undisputed king of online satire, magnificently lampooning local, national and international media. In the wake of 9/11 they were among the first to pierce the bubble of grief with some brilliantly targeted pieces (e.g. "Not Knowing What Else To Do, Woman Bakes American Flag Cake") and have managed – against the odds – to keep the comedy quotient incredibly high over the years. And, indeed, fool other newspapers into reporting their stories as fact; was Danish television station TV2 really taken in by "Sean Penn Demands To Know What Asshole Took SeanPenn@gmail.com"?

Mods and mashups

When you're using image, music or video editing software, the facility that lets you muck about with your own files obviously allows you to muck about with someone else's, too. No subterfuge necessary; you can just doodle over anyone's painstakingly assembled creations to your heart's content. For example, we know that computers are sophisticated enough to let us remove a disgraced family member from a wedding portrait. But that same skill can be redeployed to lift an image of Marilyn Manson grimacing onstage at the Chicago Allstate Arena and place him in the lineup of world leaders at the last G8 summit. Same procedure, funnier outcome.

Mods and mashups

There's a bonanza of material out there to play with. Images can be dragged to the desktop with the tweak of a mouse. Torrent sites can be ransacked for music and video – and that's before you've gone through your collections of CDs and DVDs. Digitizing your vinyl LPs or VHS cassettes and scanning pages from books is just as easy. And once it's all in the digital domain, the software that lets you manipulate this stuff is not only powerful, it's also cheap. While the program that's synonymous with image editing – Adobe Photoshop – will set you back a fair whack, there are open source software packages such as GIMP that you can grab for free and that offer many of the same features. And it's the same with music and video; sure, the best software packages can cost upwards of £500, but you can often find something online that'll meet your requirements for a fraction of the price.

We'll look at the question of whether you're actually allowed to share your modifications (or mods) and mashups a bit later (the short answer being, er, no, not really). But, regardless of the legal position, people are doing it, and there's not a great deal that can be done to stop them. While some of the creators of the links in this chapter have run up against legal trouble, others have been spurred on to more audacious deeds of digital delinquency by the overwhelming response they've received. It's worth noting that barely any of this lot are computer whizzkids; they've just come up with a good idea and run with it. The amateurishness of some of the clips only adds to their appeal – indeed, they often represent a marked improvement on the original. No wonder some copyright holders get so hot under the collar…

Guitar god parodies
tinyurl.com/yrk6vm

If any group of people need their pomposity rapidly deflating, it's smug guitar heroes who twiddle their way through interminable fretboard manoeuvres while a curiously rapt audience hangs on their every arpeggio. Santeri Ojala did this by overdubbing their live performance videos with his own atonal guitar noodlings that seem to match, finger for finger, what's being played on screen, with accompanying instruments dropping in and out depending on whether they're in view. YouTube was forced to remove the videos after complaints from humourless record companies, but they live on here thanks to wired.com.

Taz and Beefy
youtube.com/watch?v=RkoyP_fJzn0

Taz and Beefy were just two young men slightly the worse for wear at a rap event in Southwest London. But when they were approached by a cameraman for a quick vox pop about the evening, they each delivered a hair-raising fifteen seconds of amateur gold: Taz with a 200mph rap about nothing in particular and Beefy beatboxing explosively while chanting the word "Beefy". The two separate clips had already gone down a storm online, but when some glorious saint managed to combine the two together in a mashup, the results were pure genius.

Mods and mashups

Tourist guy
tinyurl.com/3dxvhv

After it was fairly quickly established that this September 11 souvenir (a photo of an unlucky tourist posing on top of the World Trade Center while an aircraft approached him from the rear) was a fake, it was open season for image editors to place the same guy in as many horrific situations as possible. His whistlestop historical tour saw him at the assassination of JFK, the Parisian Concorde crash and the Hindenburg disaster, amongst others. The Hungarian man in the picture who also created the initial Photoshop masterpiece shied away from the inevitable publicity. "It was a joke meant for my friends," he said, shamefacedly.

Hopkin green frog
lostfrog.org

Posters on lampposts come in many guises: advertisements for electroclash parties under railway arches (starts 11pm, only £6); appeals for the return of stray kittens that have sneaked out of the catflap and are now charming the entire neighbourhood; ineffective calls for NATO to withdraw troops from Afghanistan. But this plaintive plea for the return of a child's toy frog inspired creative imaginations everywhere, with magazine covers, World War II propaganda posters and faked TV news footage reworked to carry its moving message. "I'll find my frog. Who took my frog?"

Escort – all through the night
youtube.com/watch?v=qqRDct1IDl8

Combine eight DVDs of footage from *The Muppet Show*, a new single from an unashamedly retro disco act from Brooklyn, and three days of intense video editing, and you come up with this fantastic promo clip that could easily have been the brainchild of Jim Henson himself. From those strangely alluring hairy monsters to "Pigs In Space" flypasts to the energetic performances of Dr Teeth and The Electric Mayhem (with Animal thrashing away on drums, of course) it's a perfectly conceived nostalgia trip for anyone over the age of thirty.

You suck at Photoshop

youtube.com/watch?v=MWn0lxRNqos

Who better to teach you all the skills you need to doctor photos properly than a disgruntled graphic design expert who is not only witheringly contemptuous of everyone's half-baked Photoshop efforts, but who also seems to be wrestling with personal trauma after discovering that his wife is sleeping with his best friend? While these unhinged lessons are a fantastic spoof of computer tutorials, they do actually teach you something. Perfect if you're facing imminent divorce and want to know how to erase a wedding ring (pictured) from a photo of your "happy" day.

Photoshop may not be able to grant you a divorce, but at least its tools and palettes can allow you to pretend the wedding never happened – and for the fraction of a cost of a lawyer.

Recut trailers

youtube.com/watch?v=KmkVWuP_sO0

Anyone who has peeked through their fingers at Jack Nicholson in *The Shining* and sworn that they've never do it again during the hours of darkness will appreciate this trailer, which repositions the film as a cute romantic comedy. Or perhaps you find the spoonful of sugar that is *Mary Poppins* a bit sickly, and would prefer it as a horror flick (youtube.com/watch?v= 2T5_0AGdFic). There are tougher challenges for budding video editors, should they choose to accept them: maybe portraying *Jaws* as a friendly neighbourhood shark, or picking out those slapstick comedy moments from *The Passion Of The Christ*. Set to it, kids.

B3TA
b3ta.com

It may be known as the world's largest repository of male dominated puerile humour but, through sheer quantity of content generated, B3TA and its thriving community are often responsible for the best online gags in any given week. Yes, there are stories about poo; yes, in jokes render much of their messageboard totally impenetrable; and yes, new members are mercilessly savaged if they break the "rules" – but you can forgive all that for the results of each B3TA image challenge, where the web's pictures are ransacked and desecrated in order to provide amusement for the 100,000 subscribers to their weekly newsletter.

Osama meets Sesame Street
tinyurl.com/3dhjya

One Photoshop artist's somewhat futile quest to prove that Bert, the character from *Sesame Street*, is pure evil in puppet form, had the most unexpected of consequences. He spliced together a picture of Bert with another of Osama bin Laden to give the impression that the two were united in the war against

Western imperialism, and put it online; a chap in Bangladesh then downloaded the image and used it – along with many others of bin Laden – for a run of two thousand anti-USA posters. Seeing the image of Bert being earnestly waved at pro-al Qaeda rallies provided a few seconds of light relief during grim news reports about the war on terror.

Not everyone notices what's wrong with this picture at first glance – but look, there, bottom-right … it's Bert! Hilariously, neither the poster designer nor the staff at Dhaka's Placards-R-Us noticed it either.

You're the man now dog!
ytmnd.com

Trying to explain the point of YTMND is almost completely pointless – indeed, the site's creator spent more than a year trying to write the "about" page of the website, and ended up just copying a definition from Wikipedia. That would seem to give us carte blanche to do the same thing: "It's a website community that centers around the creation of YTMNDs, which are pages featuring a juxtaposition of a single image along with large zooming text and a looping sound file." Explore them at length at ytmnd.com, and marvel at the lengths to which people will go in order to raise a muted snigger from an online audience.

Image macros

The phrase "image macros" probably suggests a topic as free of excitement as the history of differential calculus or, I dunno, the chemical process behind the manufacture of gravy browning. There's certainly nothing inherently astonishing about them; they're merely photos with superimposed text. But they're responsible for some of the most virulent forms of photo sharing ever seen on the Net, and have allowed the unlikely and ungrammatical phrase "I can has cheezburger?" (pictured below) to spawn its own bastardized syntax and a slew of spin-off websites.

The blame can probably be laid at the door of "O RLY?", that useful shorthand phrase for those who can't be bothered to type "oh really?" When someone slapped said phrase on top of a bemused looking snowy owl at some point back in 2003, similar images

came thick and fast – (*hjo3. net/orly*) – all of them featuring someone or something looking either confused, smug or panic stricken. ("Oh really?" can take on many different inflections, in the same way that "Dude!" can suggest anything from revulsion to adoration.) Over the years, the rules of the image macro became refined: you have to use the Impact font, in white, with a black outline, and invariably in capital letters. And for some reason, these precise criteria only seem to make the joke funnier.

It might seem unfair of *Faildogs.com* to poke fun at the intellectual capacity of dogs, and their inability to perform the most simple tasks without messing them up. But – as is often the case – if it's cruel, it's funny.

Then came "LOLcats": image macros of cats wearing absurd expressions or in unusual situations, with text suggesting the innermost thoughts of said cats. And of course cats never attend English lessons, do they, so LOLcats quickly rewrote all the rules of spelling and grammar. The picture of a fat, expectant cat that spawned the biggest LOLcats website (*icanhascheezburger.com*) provided the inspiration for thousands of others: the cat sleeping next to a bottle of Merlot ("I iz not alcoholic I'z passionat bout wine") or the one lodged in a PC case ("I am in ur computer stealing ur Internets"). Stranger still, the forums at icanhascheezburger.com are full of people conversing in the LOLcats dialect and pretending to be cats. Some people are even translating the Bible into LOLcats. Seriously (*lolcatbible.com*).

It's probably no surprise that dogs have got in on the act with what you might call a copycat website (*ihasahotdog.com*) along with the no-frills simplicity of *faildogs.com*, but image macros have surely been taken as far as they can go with this celebration of things-supposedly-eating-other-things (*omnomnomnom.com*). As the site states, if you're not saying "Om nom nom nom" out loud while looking at the pictures, well, you're doing it wrong.

Mods and mashups

If you squint, without your glasses on, in a smoky room, at midnight, during a power cut, you might just mistake the above for Judy Garland. Behold the power of Sleeveface.

Sleeveface
sleeveface.com

"One or more persons obscuring or augmenting any part of their body or bodies with record sleeve(s) causing an illusion," reads the terse explanatory note at the top of this site – but that sums it up perfectly. Creating sleeveface images has become an addictive pastime for many, limited only by one's imagination, the size of one's record collection and having enough clothes knocking about in your wardrobe to make the final image look vaguely realistic. The combination of a Mozart sleeve with a boy wearing a football strip is a favourite, but here's a handy guide if you want to get stuck in: youtube.com/watch?v=NVt4jOasujc.

This is Sparta
youtube.com/watch?v=rZBA0SKmQy8

To active YouTube creators, there's not many film clips that can't be improved by cutting them up, superimposing heads from one film onto some bodies in another, employing low rent special effects and putting a jarring, insistent techno soundtrack behind the whole thing. Well over eleven million people found themselves culturally enriched by this particular example, which took clips of actor Gerard Butler repeatedly roaring "This is Sparta" in the film *300*, and put him into a range of situations that looked very dissimilar to the original Ancient Greek setting, such as behind the wheel of a speeding car.

This isn't Sparta, it's the brainchild of an enthusiastic young video editor: Gerard Butler gets angry in triplicate.

Battle of the album covers
youtube.com/watch?v=x6bUD9PJ6i8

Made over three months by animators Rohitash Rao and Abraham Spear, this short film features iconic album covers from rock history battling to the death. Billy Joel unleashes rapid gunfire from the cover of *52nd Street*, injuring Rick James on *Street Songs* and Eminem on *Encore*; Eminem retaliates, spilling blood on the feet of Joe Jackson's *Look Sharp*, before the women on Roxy Music's *Country Life* ride to the rescue with a salvo of missiles and radial saw blades. You get the idea. Like Sleeveface, but with artillery.

So, is all this actually legal?

The ease with which we can swipe media and perform surgery on it means that we often forget that the raw material has usually been given to the world on the understanding that it won't be copied, altered, reversed, squashed, extended or otherwise fiddled about with. But while the law still upholds copyright, the concept itself has been blown out of the water in the digital age. Filesharing is rife, attempts to prevent people from downloading online music and video are easily circumvented, and content creators are unwillingly forced into one of two camps: those who try to stop people from nicking their stuff as they believe that it damages their artistic credibility; and those who have decided that trying to fight it is more trouble than it's worth – and, in any case, surely any exposure is good exposure?

If you're a musician who has nicked a portion of another track and you want to release your handiwork commercially, you're obliged to "clear" the sample by approaching the copyright holder and negotiating a deal. But on the Internet, there's no presiding judge, no pressing plant who'll refuse to handle your music if you don't have the necessary permission. It might not be legal, but uploading your creation is a piece of cake. So ingenious mashups of two or more existing tracks have become incredibly popular online, and underground acclaim can occasionally force the tracks back into the mainstream: the story behind the creation of Sugababes' "Freak like Me" is one of the best known examples (*tinyurl.com/2usgkv*)

Photos are even easier to swipe and doctor. Flickr, the photo sharing site favoured by many talented amateur photographers, is a quick and easy image source for unscrupulous picture trawlers, and even the picture desks of print media – who should know better – have been caught pilfering. But again, enforcing your copyright is a nightmare; an eagle eye is your only weapon, and the chances of you accidentally stumbling across an instance of your work being used are almost nil. As a result, many choose to share their work under various "Creative Commons" licenses, which permit usage under certain stipulated conditions – perhaps for non-commercial purposes only, or only with a specified picture credit. But you're still reliant on goodwill. And there's not a great deal of it about.

Most people get away with their mods and mashups until they either start reaching some level of notoriety or start

If you're looking for pictures, music or video that you can use without worrying about lawsuits, the easily navigated creativecommons.org website is a good place to start your search.

making money, at which point writs start to fly. In America you can defend yourself on the grounds of satire or parody, as long as you can prove that your creation could "reasonably be perceived as commenting on the original or criticizing it to some degree". But in the UK there's no such allowance for satire, and in any case the sheer cost of fighting a case means that most people will remove their creation from the Internet just to stop threats of legal action landing on the doormat. When Prince's lawyers contacted members of B3TA after they'd doctored images of him, the site's owners were quick to remove them, just for a quiet life. But there's no doubt that the days of universal respect for copyright are over. The advice to copyright holders from Rob Manuel, founder of B3TA, is tongue-in-cheek but all too true: if you don't want to have your creations reworked, don't put them online.

This grotesque combination of a kitten and a "spongmonkey" breathed new life into an indie-rock classic, thanks to Joel Veitch.

Kittens singing The Vines
rathergood.com/vines

Joel Veitch would probably never put himself up there with the greatest animators of all time, but with the primitive Flash software at his disposal, a keen eye for surreality and an image library full of cute animals, his work has become instantly recognizable. There's not the slightest attempt at making anything look realistic; its charm comes purely from its joyful, two-dimensional stupidity. The viral fame of many of Veitch's clips saw his ideas being nicked by a multinational soft drinks company, amongst others; but they settled out of court, and he now makes adverts for products as varied as train journeys and credit cards.

Pimp that snack

pimpthatsnack.com/projects.php

It's all very well sitting at a computer and unleashing your creative skills using a piece of pirated software, but what about the people who actually get their hands dirty? Pete Wilcock from Manchester recreates the world's pre-packaged snack foods in enormous, home made versions using standard store cupboard ingredients; some, like the giant Toffee Crisp (illustrated right), look good enough to eat – albeit with the help of several hungry friends – while the spam fritter is more of a candidate for being pushed gently to the side of a giant sized plate using a suitably colossal fork.

Darth Vader being annoying

youtube.com/watch?v=7YwLQSTo_ow

This lovely cut up of a scene from *The Empire Strikes Back* recasts Darth Vader as a petulant teen who keeps retreating back into his mechanical podule and in doing so prevents General Veers giving him an important update on the ongoing assault on the planet Hoth. "What is it, General?" "My Lord, the fleet has moved out of light speed; Comscan has detected an energy field–" Veers, despite having a good few attempts, doesn't get any further than this thanks to Vader's newly found sense of mischief.

How to: make a Photoshop headswap

What better way to demonstrate the power of Photoshop than to graft Chairman Mao's head onto the body of a kitten? Here, we're actually going to use Photoshop Elements – a cheaper version of the industry image-editing standard – but the technique should work with most image editing applications.

Your first step is to hunt for two decent quality images. The easiest place to look is Google Image Search (*images.google.com*); a quick search for "Mao" and "kitten" yields up plenty of source material.

Open up both files in Elements. Now you need to superimpose the chairman's head onto the image of the kitten. There are many ways to skin a cat (pun kind-of intended) but in this case, the easiest way is to use the the lasso tool to draw roughly around Mao's head. When you've done that, you can quickly decapitate him by using the arrow tool to drag and drop him in the vicinity of the kitten.

But hang on, hang on. This falls some way short of being a cultural revolution – not least because Mao's head is bigger than the kitten's. So the next step is to resize the head so that it fits nicely on the cat's body. If you go to the Edit menu and then to Transform>Scale, you can drag one of the handles on the corners of his head. And, if you also hold down the shift key, this will keep the proportions correct and stop Mao either gaining or losing a considerable amount of weight. (If you can't see the corner handles, try zooming out a bit using the magnifying glass tool.)

Now, this arrangement of Mao and a kitten is never going to look particularly natural, but the least you can do is to try and grade his face into the fur in order to smoothen things out a little. You can achieve this in two ways: either with the rubber stamp tool, or the spot healing brush. The rubber stamp (the lower of the two icons shown here) allows you to select an area of the image (hold down the alt key to do this) and then paint that part of the image onto another area. The spot healing brush works in a similar way, except you don't need to select an area to copy – it automatically

selects texture from the surrounding area and blends it with the bit you're painting. (Fussing with brush opacity and hardness should help get the effect you're after.) Now you just have to save the image as a Web-ready JPG file – and hey presto: your very own Chairman Miaow.

Spinning a leek

leekspin.info

There's no conceivable reason why this clip should have been as popular as it was, unless its hypnotic qualities just sent everyone into a blissful and unquestioning trance. It's a four-frame clip of a Japanese cartoon character twirling a leek (or a spring onion, or a scallion, depending on your nationality) with a gibberish verse from a Finnish folk song in the background. No one has

dared to come forward to claim the credit for this one, but it was hugely popular. "Yaa tsi tsup ari dik ari dull an dik ari dill an dits tan dool la dippyduppy dull la roop uttyroopy la goorigan gook aya gittygangool." Altogether now!

Anime-influenced rotation of root vegetables was generally considered a niche pursuit until this viral swept across the Internet.

Buffalax

youtube.com/watch?v=ZA1NoOOoaNw

There are probably more useful things a boy could do with his time than go through songs on old Bollywood videos, write down the English words that approximate to the Hindi lyrics, and then upload the newly subtitled version to YouTube. Keeping stick insects, perhaps. Or collecting sea shells. But several million have watched Buffalax's creations and digested such magical poetry as: "All of them like the bun, now poop on them Oliver. Oh, daddy." Despite prominent warnings that this is not the official translation in the comments section, slightly stupid people still ponder deeply over hidden meanings.

Animal magnetism

As we saw in the previous chapter, if there's a golden rule of the Internet, it's that people love kittens. We can't get enough kitten action. And if we can't find enough kittens, we can move on to cats, then dogs, and then ferrets, and when we've run out of domesticated animals there's a whole menagerie of other lifeforms to seek out – reptilian, amphibian, mammalian – not to mention all the subtitled pets, energetic cartoons and terrifying hybrids knocked up using Photoshop that we've already encountered in previous chapters. And if it were possible to slump exhausted and dishevelled over the finishing line of the Internet, having gorged yourself silly on cute, doe-eyed creatures, it's guaranteed that, even

then, a kitten would pop up and bat you repeatedly on the side of the nose to a relentlessly pulsating Euro-trance soundtrack.

If your tolerance levels for this kind of thing are particularly low – and who could blame you? – you'd begrudgingly have to admit that, bearing in mind the rather grim history of humans using animals for their own entertainment, the magnificent cyberzoo that lies before us on the Internet is reassuringly benign. Online poker and roulette sites are booming in popularity, but opportunities to put credit card bets on live cockfighting are noticable by their absence. And amid the thousands of video clips of animals up to various antics, you'll only see a dancing bear tied to a stick if it's advertising a compassionate campaign for the Wildlife Trust of India. No, our most celebrated Internet stars from the animal kingdom include otters who enjoy holding hands with other otters and cats that bear an uncanny resemblance to world leaders. Cuteness, rather than exploitation, is the order of the day – and our response is generally to go "Aaaah".

Many of the most popular animal related virals are video clips that would be equally at home on TV shows called "Slapstick Tortoises" or "The Big Budgie Laugh-in", where someone happened to have a video camera switched on at the precise moment that, say, a dog failed to notice that the patio doors were closed, or a cat attacked a fruitbowl for no apparent reason. But other animals show themselves to be vastly more talented than any television antecedents such as Skippy the Bush Kangaroo (who jumped and made clicking noises) or Champion the Wonder Horse (who merely ran quite fast). Later we'll encounter a dog with an impressive aptitude for skateboarding, a cat playing the piano, and a shrimp keeping fit; of course, Rover, Tibbles and Shrimpy aren't remotely aware that they've achieved the level of fame that they have, and for them there'll be no big Paris Hilton-style cash-in, no chat show circuit, no trashy magazine exposés of them emerging from seedy nightclubs. But that's what makes the viral stars of this chapter particularly distinguished: animals have no vanity. They're not trying to show off. They're not driven by hit counters, or the rapidly changing tastes of the online community. They're just being themselves. And on the Internet, that's almost unheard of.

Beedogs
beedogs.com

Dogs have precious little interest in being more like bees. The tax advantages are minimal, the hours depressingly long and the whole notion of "going for a walk" disappears out of the window. But one particular group of Internet users believe that a dog's aura is enormously enhanced by taking a leaf or two out of a bee's personal style manual. Hence Beedogs, "the premier online repository for pictures of dogs in bee costumes". You can now browse dozens of images of dogs wearily indulging their unhinged owners' canine-apian fantasies while experiencing great sadness and pity.

Dogs were once considered to be "man's best friend" until we started dressing them up as insects. They are thought to be preparing to retaliate.

Dramatic chipmunk
youtube.com/watch?v=a1Y73sPHKxw

Firstly, it's not a chipmunk, it's a prairie dog. But as a prairie dog isn't actually a dog (it's a rodent), let's call it a chipmunk – either to avoid or add to the confusion, depending on your point of view. Secondly, at five seconds long it's one of the briefest clips on YouTube, and also one of the most popular – probably

because people watch it two or three times to achieve maximum chipmunk-based satisfaction. The plot: our hero turns and stares at the camera to the sound of a stinger from the film *Young Frankenstein*. That's it. Alternative versions, cut to the themes from *James Bond* or *Kill Bill*, are also widely available.

Pelican eats pigeon
youtube.com/watch?v=QNNI_uWmQXE

The title "Pelican eats pigeon" doesn't really do this clip justice; as a feat of swallowing it surpasses any cream cracker eating contest. A defenceless bird is scooped up in the bill of a pelican in London's St James's Park, and after a brief struggle which looks like an escapologist trying to fight his way out of a sack the pigeon eventually resigns itself to being slowly consumed, and the pelican resigns itself to waddling down to the chemist for some indigestion tablets. Ironic footnote unappreciated by pigeons everywhere: the action takes place in front of a sign saying "Do Not Feed The Pelicans".

Battle at Kruger
youtube.com/watch?v=LU8DDYz68kM

You're out for a leisurely walk with your parents when you suddenly find yourself as a potential main course for a pride of lions. Then you end up in a tug-of-grub between said lions and a hungry crocodile. Your parents then reappear with a load of their mates to try and get you back. No, it's not a horrific and nightmarish visit to the zoo, but a life-shaping experience for a baby buffalo at South Africa's Kruger National Park that was captured in a seven-minute film by Jason Schlosberg and David Budzinski while on holiday. If you don't want the ending spoiled, look away now: the butler did it.

Shrimp running on a treadmill with the Benny Hill theme
youtube.com/watch?v=cMO8Pyi3UpY

This video, the contents of which are described pretty accurately in the title, asks many more questions than it answers. Does this man actually keep a shrimp as a pet? Or was he just having some fun with it before putting it in a delicious gumbo for his dinner? What possible reason could he admit to for having a miniature underwater treadmill to hand? And, more importantly, why does the theme tune to the *Benny Hill Show* (it's called "Yakety Sax", in case you were wondering) seem to enhance footage of anything running fast?

Animal magnetism

Cute overload
cuteoverload.com

It was the Ancient Greeks who first remarked that beauty was in the eye of the beholder. Web surfers, however, have decided that beauty is a fluffy ball of sickening cuteness with big eyes and a doleful expression. If you're the kind of person who looks at a guinea pig and thinks "I wuv you. I weally, weally wuv you," then Megan Frost's terrifyingly popular Cute Overload site is for you. If, however, your feelings for guinea pigs are at best ambivalent, then check out the polar opposite uglyoverload. blogspot.com where the balance is redressed with a fearsome showcase of Mother Nature's off days.

Floating dog
youtube.com/watch?v=REI64B2oB1U

Putting a plane into a steep dive allows those within the aircraft to experience temporary weightlessness. In this video, the pilot and copilot are sensibly strapped into their seats, but they appear to have forgotten about their dog who, up until the moment of the dive, had been quietly snoozing in the back. Most of us would feel confused and disorientated in an anti-grav situation, so imagine what it's like for poor Rover, who hovers upside down in mid-air, along with various bits of debris in the cockpit, before the plane levels off and his airborne adventure comes to an abrupt end.

Fainting goats
youtube.com/watch?v=we9_CdNPuJg

We take our ability to run away from danger for granted. If you're confronted by a knife wielding hoodlum or a fast moving juggernaut, your instinct is to flee, rather than quietly lie down on the floor and await serious injury. Sadly, for a particular breed of goats in Marshall County, Tennessee, a genetic mutation has forced them them to take the latter option; the slightest rush of adrenalin renders them completely immobile (pictured right). They may have drawn the evolutionary short straw, but the citizens of Marshall County honour their beloved goats with a festival every year being careful, of course, not to make it too exciting.

Getting their own back

Frisky donkey
youtube.com/watch?v=rCMB0scm9nw

You know that a home video clip has reached a certain level of popularity when it's seized by a South American television station and "amusing" voices are dubbed over the top in order to up the comedy quotient. Anyway, the story goes that a man attempted to relieve himself in a field,

Social petworking

Websites such as MySpace, Facebook, Bebo and Friendster give us an impressive latticework of online contacts. We can connect to our existing friends and make new ones, find people who are equally fond of *Battlestar Galactica*, send them messages, adorn their profiles with flattering comments and keep track of how their driving lessons are going (not that well, now that you mention it). If that didn't already take up far too much of our time, web entrepreneurs have now enabled us to do the whole thing all over again, but this time on behalf of our pets.

Dogster.com, for example, contains profiles for approaching 400,000 pet dogs, with thousands of new ones added every day. But while human social networks reveal our incredible diversity, our distinct personalities and our questionable sense of humour, dog profiles merely reveal that dogs like running, eating and sleeping. Few dogs admit to having any kind of fondness for the symphonies of Shostakovich. Alarmingly, many of the doggy profiles are written in the first person, conjuring up an image of a dog sitting at a computer and composing detailed blog entries about the enjoyment and pleasure he derived from running around in the snow. Dogster, to their credit, try to remind the humans behind the profiles that they're not actually dogs by involving them in forum discussions with other humans, albeit with a slightly odd slant – "Do you love your vet?" No, not really. "Do you eat dog food?" Er, no. No, I don't eat dog food.

Catster.com comes from the same stable as Dogster; membership figures are lower, but hey, you know how difficult cats can be to pin down. While we know that we can choose our friends, and we can't choose our friends' friends, we can most definitely choose our cat's friends. Indeed, pet based social networking depends on us imagining that our snooty Siamese would get along famously with a domestic longhaired moggy from Bilbao. The ridiculously named *hamsterster.com* has now joined in on the act – although the site owner has to stress persistently that it's not a joke, no, it's a real site, and yes, gerbils are allowed as members. Most pet networking sites – *fuzzster.com*, *mypetfriends.biz*, *petster. com* – welcome all species, especially if they're fluffy, although *pet-files.com* has a section devoted to pet apes. No pet apes appear in this section, but that's probably better than there being one solitary, slightly depressed ape.

All this palaver, of course, is just a smokescreen for barely concealed flirting between pet owners, who believe that owning a similarly shaped, similarly sized pet is as good a basis for a successful, loving relationship as any other – and who's to say that they're not correct? One site makes no bones about it: "Whether you are looking for romance or a breeding partner, *petspassions.com* is the site for you." (I think they mean pet breeding.) But one does wonder, while these people are busy pretending to be their pets, whether bored cats and dogs all over the world are considering launching a class action for negligence.

but was interrupted by an inquisitive donkey. Cue several minutes of farcical cat and mouse action during which, for some reason, the gentleman seems utterly unconcerned about pulling his trousers up. The donkey sees his laidback, almost cavalier attitude to nudity as some kind of invitation, with predictable consequences.

Baby and cobra
youtube.com/watch?v=mEVq_fGsY-o

I'm not a gambling man, but in a face off between a three-metre long cobra and a toddler with no trousers, my money's on the long, thin fellow with the scaly skin. Watch the fearless baby provoke the snake into spasms of rage – if you can bear it. It's hard to justify the carefree laughter from the child's family as the cobra wraps itself around the baby's neck, but the comments posted below the various instances of this video on YouTube are irritatingly righteous. Maybe they'll be brought together in a book called *The Misspelled, Racist, Expletive Ridden Guide To Modern Parenting*.

Horse dumps on children's entertainer
youtube.com/watch?v=hBsPi5sCerU

It's an old television maxim that you should never work with children and animals, and this is particularly sound advice if either the child or the animal needs the toilet. British readers may remember the carnage that ensued in the BBC's *Blue Peter* studio when an elephant chose to express itself fecally on the floor during a live broadcast, but at least the *Blue Peter* presenters were sensible enough not to put their heads through the animal's hind legs and shout "Peek a boo!" That, sadly, is what happens here, and the horse grabs the opportunity to pass commentary on the state of contemporary television.

Oh look, they're just like us

Butt-smelling monkey
youtube.com/watch?v=V51lNCWtWLQ

Any unpleasant discoveries we make about our own bodies – the taste of earwax, the nonchalant ease with which you can wet yourself – are usually made at a very young age, and rarely during a geography exam, or while taking your date to a French restaurant, or accepting an Oscar for best original screenplay. This poor monkey, however, had the misfortune to have one such epiphany in front of a television camera, ensuring that his moment of horror would circulate on the Internet for generations, thus educating our children, and our children's children, about the unpleasant aroma of a primate's bottom.

Sneezing panda
youtube.com/watch?v=FzRH3iTQPrk

For a few seconds, you don't even notice the baby panda lying on its front on the floor; you're distracted by the giant one sitting in the corner – presumably its mum – munching thoughtfully on a sandwich (okay, it's probably bamboo, but I like to think it's a sandwich). And then the baby panda's mucous membranes get irritated: cue explosive noise, a startled mother, and several million satisfied Internet users. Combining the comedic potential of a sneeze with a baby animal and the perpertual mystery of the Orient was bound to result in a copper-bottomed viral hit.

"Do you see us getting married?"
"Sure... maybe we could get a little cottage in the country..."
"Mmm."
"A garden..."
"That would be nice."
"A couple of kids, a dog..."
"A dog??"
"No, actually, you're right, best forget about the dog."

Otters holding hands
youtube.com/watch?v=epUk3T2Kfno

It's reassuring when other species show some kind of romantic affection towards each other, as it makes us feel slightly less appalled at spending good money on a dozen red roses, a Hallmark gift card or a dirty weekend in Rhyl. This clip of two otters slowly floating around an aquarium in Vancouver while apparently holding hands certainly has a marked effect on the woman doing the filming, who repeatedly utters the words "adorable" despite there being the distinct possibility that this could be the otters' way of settling vicious disputes over territory.

Skateboarding dog
youtube.com/watch?v=CQzUsTFqtW0

You can put anything onto a skateboard, shove it along the ground and upload a video of it to YouTube. Skateboarding lasagne, perhaps. But Tillman the skateboarding dog has won a global audience of millions because, well, he's got way more technique than a lasagne. He rides that skateboard as casually as a commuter riding an escalator, before picking up speed and negotiating corners with consummate skill. "It's not a trick," says Tillman's proud owner, "it's a lifestyle." As yet, no footage exists of Tillman doing an inward heelflip (whatever that might be) but it's surely only a matter of time.

Masturbating kangaroo
youtube.com/watch?v=DoKrMW8giGg

Self-pleasure is an intensely private activity. At least, it is for human beings, who carry the weight of several millenia of almost biblical shame at such dispicable habits. Animals, however, couldn't care less whether you're watching or not, and our fascination with these bold, frenetic displays is evident on the Internet; it's particularly notable that when I went looking for this clip, I had to wade through several other clips of kangaroos masturbating in order to get to the right one. Now can I have my mind replaced, please, mine is soiled now. Thanks.

Virtual fluffiness

If you don't much like the idea of animal hair coating your sofa, or flushing your third successive goldfish down the toilet after it has met its maker, it's still possible to experience some of the pleasure of owning a pet without all the associated unpredictability, nasty odours and death. The Japanese invented handheld, electronic Tamagotchi pets back in the mid 1990s, and succeeded in emotionally bonding a generation of children to a beeping device powered by a watch battery. Quite some achievement. But nothing in comparison to the colossal popularity of virtual pets; the largest site, *neopets. com*, contains some 226 million imaginary pets, ranking the equally imaginary land of Neopia where all said pets "live" as somewhere between Indonesia and Brazil in terms of population.

Some people claim that virtual pets are a vast improvement on their carbon-based counterparts, as pixels on a screen can never suffer from neglect; if your virtual pet's hunger meter is in the red, you're fairly unlikely to get a knock at the door from an animal rights

The World of Neopia

All the fun of having a pet, at a fraction of the cost and without having to empty a litter tray: welcome to the online menagerie that is neopets.com. And aside from the whole animals angle, it also happens to be one of the best-looking websites around.

organisation demanding your immediate arrest. But as we're all fully aware, real animals don't have hunger meters, or satisfaction ratings – so do virtual pets really prepare kids for owning real ones, as is often claimed? What they certainly manage to do is keep children's attention: Neopets in particular is consistently rated as one of the "stickiest" websites on the Internet – it will keep you clicking around its many pages for hours on end.

It's pretty simple to create your own artificial companion; within a couple of minutes on neopets.com I'd created a cute yellow spherical ball of fur, which I immediately and affectionately named Trevor Nympton. Trevor is a town dwelling creature, who enjoys reading, learning and making new friends, and thanks to a shopping spree in the Neopets shopping mall, is now the proud owner of a "Sweetheart Ballgown" and an "Air Faerie Bubble Necklace". (Trevor's not confused about his sexuality, he's just experimenting.) The whims of these virtual pets are kept satisfied by buying food with credits that you earn from playing a range of online games, many of which are horribly addictive and would undoubtedly distract you from your pet's well being, if your computer didn't persistently remind you of any imminent starvation issues.

I'm not sure how Trevor is doing, these days. The idea that he has somehow withered away and died in my absence from the website is quite distressing. Other sites such as *powerpets.com* have anticipated this, and operate a system whereby if you're not logged in, time miraculously stands still and your pet is kind of cryogenically frozen until you come back. From a tactile point of view, the act of stroking a gently purring cat could never really be replaced by putting a cursor over a cute object on a screen and repeatedly hammering your mouse – and in that respect the world of virtual pets is curiously dissatisfying. But if you're allergic to cats, well, it's a positive boon.

Cats

Bacon attached to cat

scalzi.com/whatever/004457

An award-winning novelist posts his to-do list on his blog, with a slightly surreal bullet point – "tape bacon to the cat" – as a whimsical aside. His readership challenge him to follow through on his promise. He calls his wife for permission to do so. His wife wearily grants him permission, on the understanding that the bacon is removed immediately after photographic proof has been captured. This accomplished writer (who also happens to be the author of *The Rough Guide To The Universe*) tapes bacon to his cat, and is inundated with comments of either approval, derison, or concern about the hygiene implications.

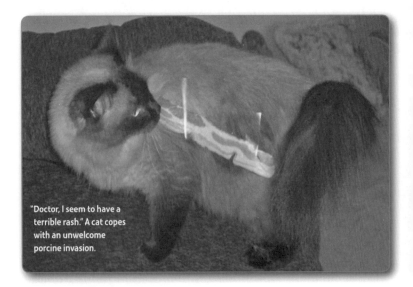

"Doctor, I seem to have a terrible rash." A cat copes with an unwelcome porcine invasion.

Practice makes purr-fect

youtube.com/watch?v=TZ860P4iTaM

Nora is a cat who plays the piano. Warning: don't get your hopes up for anything more than a lopsided, drunken version of "Chopsticks"; Nora does not, after all, have the ten-digit advantage possessed by, say, Liberace. Having said that, she does caress the keys with a sensitivity that parents of youngsters grappling with their first scales and arpeggios can only dream of. After her initial online hit, Nora was coaxed out of the litter tray for two sequels – and, if you enjoy her freestyle doodlings, there's a CD available of her playing with a jazz band, who should be called Cats Waller, but aren't.

Kittenwar! May the cutest kitten win!

kittenwar.com

Top-notch interactive kitten fun, albeit slightly repetitive: choose the cutest of two kitten pictures, and then … do it again. Kitten naming conventions are laid bare, here, with a series of monikers that no one would want to start shouting in rough neighbourhoods should their cat ever get lost: Nutmeg, Cuddles, Bitsy, Bongo, Wanker … (I made up the last one). The makers of this site have recently started an offshoot, catsinsinks. com, the contents of which will not come as much of a surprise. Rumours about the launch of "rabbitsinkettles.com", however, have been dismissed as pure speculation.

Animal magnetism

Another unsuspecting moggy becomes forever ensnared in the laptop labyrinth.

The infinite cat project
infinitecat.com

Someone posts a picture of their cat, Frankie, on an online forum. Someone else posts a picture of their cat looking at this picture of Frankie. A chap called Mike Stanfill posts a picture of his cat, Poozy, looking at the picture of the cat looking at Frankie. And because it's the Internet, the whole thing gets out of control. Stanfill's website now holds more than 1500 cats, forming the initial section of what one fears may truly become an infinite chain. The only way of breaking said chain would be if Frankie laid eyes on any one of these pictures, at which point the universe would probably snap shut like a mousetrap.

Cats that look like Hitler
catsthatlooklikehitler.com

Our distate for Hitler's country-invading behaviour has consigned the toothbrush moustache to the dustbin of history. If, as a grown man, you're misguided enough to grow one, you'll never look suave, dashing or elegant. You'll look like Hitler. But while humans have a choice, cats that are born with a dark patch under their nose are forever destined to remind their owners of a Nazi. A gallery of some two thousand "kitlers" has been assembled here; if you think it's all in questionable taste, the fact that the cats are blissfully ignorant of twentieth century history might provide some small consolation.

"I modelled my look on Charlie Chaplin. Seriously, I'm a huge fan of *The Gold Rush*. And I don't have the slightest intention of invading Poland, at least for the time being."

Stuff on my cat
stuffonmycat.com

"Do you like putting stuff on your cat?" asked Mario Garza, somewhat tentatively, on his website back in the spring of 2005. While delivering such a line in a singles bar might well be a recipe for instant humiliation, on the Internet it's like asking people if they like envelopes full of cash sellotaped to boxes of chocolates. Every hour of every day you'll see a new mog sitting under the weight of something or other – food, technology, general detritus … For a very similar web experience, visit stuffonmymutt.com. Web entrepreneurs note: "stuffonmymum. com" has not yet been registered.

Rico loves Jefferson
youtube.com/watch?v=2pqkJD6uCcY

"Is it really so wrong?" whispered Rico into Jefferson's ear. "We're both mammals, after all." Jefferson wriggled free of Rico's grasp for what must have been the thirteenth time that day. "So are bats and blue whales," said Jefferson, "but I don't see them trying to hump each other in the corridor." Rico stared into the middle distance, wistfully. "This is surely the love that dare not speak its name," he said, "and I hope that, one day, love between a cat and a dog will be…" Rico's soliloquy was rudely interrupted by Jefferson's furious hissing. "Look, get off my back or I'll claw your face off, you randy bastard."

Marketing and money

7

Millions of us spend inordinate amounts of time aimlessly browsing for something or other, we've no idea what. We just sit there, mouse in one hand, fizzy drink in the other, randomly clicking around, more or less on the verge of addiction; in doing so we've turned ourselves into a captive audience – perfect candidates for receiving some kind of sales pitch. If it's done well, we'll absorb any message you choose to chuck in our direction. Baboon underwear? Go on then, I'll have a dozen. And you can reach us for a fraction of the cost of putting that message on TV, on the radio, in the cinema or in newspapers. There's money to be made, here. Loads of money. Right?

Marketing and money

Well, the dotcom slump of 2000 and 2001 made it abundantly clear that the Internet economy doesn't guarantee untold riches. But when every blog goes up, when every plan for a new website is sketched out on the back of a packet of cigarettes, the dream is that it'll result in a cash bonanza. This might be done directly, by simply trying to persuade us to buy something. Sometimes it'll be a window on someone's talent, which they hope will eventually lead to international fame and flowers in their dressing room. Sometimes it's a project where, purely because human beings could conceivably be interested in it, its creators immediately imagine that everyone will be willing to hurl cash in their direction (take a bow, umpteen failed social networking websites).

But, nevertheless, the Web is an integral part of trying to sell stuff. Marketing departments love the fact that it can tell them exactly how many people see each message, exactly how many were interested enough to click through to find out more, and how many actually ended up buying something as a result. No product is launched, no film or record released, no company established without something or other being uploaded to the Web. Sometimes the results are incredibly slick, as carefully designed and assembled as the products themselves. More often, they have comparatively low rent production values in order to try and blend seamlessly with those virals that are already taking the Internet by storm. Sometimes the campaigns even go as far as masquerading as a blogger or video maker unassociated with the product; sometimes this works brilliantly, but sometimes it's horribly misconceived and the company behind it is exposed to ridicule across the Net. As with anything you put online, you've got to be braced for a storm of criticism if things don't go your way.

Advertising and marketing via such an unregulated medium as the Internet is only going to get more invasive, with increasingly distracting, insidious and ultimately annoying methods used to force us to take notice – with spam email being the most obvious example. And in this chapter we'll see that the most effective techniques are when the line between entertaining us and trying to sell us something is blurred – often to the point where we don't even notice the line at all.

Guinness riddles
guinnesstipping.com

You might remember *Myst*, one of the most popular computer games of the 1990s, in which you moved back and forth throughout an eerie landscape trying to solve a series of impenetrable puzzles in order to establish the secret of how some race called the D'ni were able to time travel using a few books. This Web-based adventure is not dissimilar, except your ultimate quest was presumably to discover that Guinness is a lip smacking dark stout with a creamy head and distinctive flavour. The code was eventually cracked (juanramon.pbwiki.com). The reward? To see a Guinness commercial! Hooray!

Trojan games
trojangames.co.uk

It's not an easy task to put together a tasteful advertising campaign for condoms that keeps sexual references to a minimum and stops short of offending prudish letter writers to right-wing newspapers. So when

Marketing and money

Trojan launched their range of warrior grade prophylactics in the UK, they just abandoned any notion of adhering to standards of decency and went straight for the big blue vein with the Trojan Games. This was a fictitious tournament held in Romania that featured unlikely sexual challenges, such as somersaulting directly, as seen here, into the reverse missionary position. Ouch.

If you could scrawl something on the side of George W Bush's aeroplane, what would it be? Marc Ecko restrained himself from using rude words, and went with "Still Free" – you can see the shots for yourself on the stillfree.com website.

Tagging Air Force One
stillfree.com

Fashion entrepreneur and relentless self-publicist Marc Ecko could always have arranged some kind of rally to protest against restrictions on free speech in the USA, but he thought – quite rightly – that a home-made video of him scaling a fence and spraying graffiti on the side of the presidential jet *Air Force One* would create more of stir. No less than three denials emerged from the Pentagon before Ecko revealed what he actually did: hire a Boeing aircraft, have it painted identically to *Air Force One* and then film himself putting graffiti on that. Which, some might say, was actually more difficult.

Cadbury's gorilla
youtube.com/watch?v=TnzFRV1Lwlo

By the end of 2006 Cadbury's weren't exactly flavour of the month after a series of product recalls and PR blunders. Quite why they chose to try and turn things around by putting an actor into a gorilla suit and have him playing drums along with Phil Collins' "In The Air Tonight" is a secret known only to those attending that surreal marketing meeting – but it certainly worked. Six million views across various video sharing websites saw sales of Dairy Milk increase, Phil Collins' bank balance swell even further, and a lucky competition winner bag a year's supply of bananas. Oh, and chocolate, obviously.

As not seen on TV

The vast majority of advertising ideas never make it anywhere near our television screens. Some are almost impulsively self-censored before they've even made it from the brains of the creative team and onto a piece of paper. Others might get chucked out on the whim of a senior executive who's just had a row with their partner over breakfast. Even the ones that are written, filmed and edited might not even make it to the final campaign, and the few that do are subjected to the kind of rigorous scrutiny that normal television programmes manage to escape. While a gag about terrorism might conceivably form the centrepiece of a topical comedy sketch show, try and sell a car using that potent combination of suicide bombings and humour, and you can be pretty sure that it won't get shown (*youtube.com/watch?v=arfNofxBtfY*).

At least, such ads won't get shown on TV. But the ease with which videos can now be shared on the Internet means that adverts that hit the cutting room floor, or were rejected by the censors, or were hurriedly pulled from the small screen after a tiny minority of self-proclaimed moral guardians wrote to complain to some official body – these can all now have a permanent home online and finally have the potential to reach an audience. As a result, you even get the feeling that ads are getting made that would never stand a chance of appearing in the traditional media, purely because the Web provides that catch-all safety net that means the work won't go to waste.

Most of the offending ads feature sex or death. But mainly death. This video of a Dodge Nitro firing off an electronic death ray in order to kill a small dog that dares to urinate on its wheels was unlikely to find favour among dog lovers (*tinyurl.com/yrcjs3*). Some might feel that actually carbonizing the poor canine rather than gently stunning him was taking things too far. Others – including, one presumes,

the maker of the ad – probably feel that it's precisely this detail that hammers home the point that you don't dare piss on a Dodge. Meanwhile, this Wendy's ad for a spicy chicken sandwich (*youtube.com/ watch?v=9zwn134_ KDk*) saw a lab assistant cast in a real life version of Beaker from *The Muppet Show*, and be reduced to a pile of molten flesh by the power of the jalapeno chilles. Wendy's, however, didn't feel that it promoted the more positive aspects of their burger.

In that post-modern, slightly cannibalistic fashion, even existing Internet virals are used as the basis for ads that, once again, never had much chance of being shown on anything other than a computer screen: the famous Mentos and Diet Coke experiments (which we'll look at in the next chapter) were recreated for this Carlsberg ad, albeit with a slightly unexpected and grisly ending (*youtube.com/ watch?v=JM2PelbGCyg*). We can also get to see ads from yesteryear that were a bit off-colour back then, but are utterly reprehensible today – like this one for Calvin Klein (*youtube.com/watch?v= vZVk21Pco-c*). Unbelievable.

For more ads you shouldn't show your grandchildren or grandmothers, point your mouse at *bestrejectedadvertising.com* and *illegaladvertising.com*.

Marketing and money

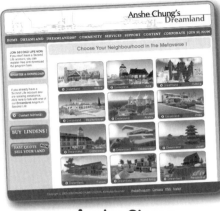

Everyone's dream of making something out of nothing was beautifully realized by Anshe Chung's million-dollar online emporium.

Anshe Chung
dreamland.anshechung.com

The concept of Second Life is hard enough to grasp. An alternate reality? But what can you do there? Simulate disco dancing with overweight men who are pretending to be attractive women? Dress up as a superhero and cavort with Tinkerbell on a urine soaked mattress in a jail cell? But why? What's even harder to get one's head around is that people are making money. Pretend money, but pretend money that can be converted into real money. And Anshe Chung (that's her Second Life name, not her real one) is the first person to make a million dollars entirely through virtual means. I'd try it myself, but one life of disappointment and failure is quite enough, thanks very much.

Quiksilver surfers
youtube.com/watch?v=6xfBNxNds0Q

There aren't that many opportunities to go surfing on urban waterways; not much in the way of waves, and always the danger of being apprehended by your local Marine Police Unit. In this video, however, the intrepid boarders chuck a stick of dynamite into the water from a bridge in order to give their colleagues something to work with. Of course, it's not what it seems: firstly it's an ad for Quiksilver, a brand of leisure clothing; secondly, while there was an explosion, it didn't create the waves – those were filmed on a nearby beach. And the professional footage was degraded to make it look like it had come from a mobile phone. Expensive, but effective.

Flea market Montgomery
youtube.com/watch?v=FJ3oHpup-pk

No secondhand furniture store has picked up quite as much publicity as Sammy Stephens' flea market in Montgomery, Alabama, thanks to an amateurish video which, for a while, laid claim to be the worst advert ever made. Until, that is, people started appreciating its hidden qualities. Sammy's rap is pretty repetitive and frequently attemps to rhyme the word "bedrooms" with "dinettes", but you've never seen a hard sell quite like it. Stopping short of creating a dance from appreciation of coffee tables and footstools might have been a good idea, but hey, I know nothing about furniture. Unlike Sammy.

Big ad
youtube.com/watch?v=891pmKoKGE4

Without the Internet, we'd never get to see those inspired moments of advertising that only appeared on the TV screens of distant lands. Not much point in running a TV ad for an Australian beer in Britain or the US, where you can't actually buy the beer. But that doesn't mean we can't appreciate genius when we see it; the response to this brilliant ad for Carlton Draught lager – initially streamed via a website before being shown on TV – was colossal, with over a million views in 132 countries within the first 24 hours. Carlton still don't sell much beer outside Australia, though.

Homemade by Da Man (me).

"Sometimes as a DJ I have these golden moments when everything seems to flow. You never know when they are going to happen, it's funny, on this particular occasion I wasn't thinking about DJing at all, but about a sweet girl I once met at a bus station."

STÜWE CLUB

Gig at Stüwe Club: "I don't know how many times I've gigged here, but they sure have good pineapple drinks (afterwards)."

My team: Rashy, Me (middle) and Roccy.

In the heat of the night: Fine-tuning volume.

"This is my home site for all home boys and home chicks, giving U a flava of the Super Greg concept." Despite the lo-fi appearance, it's also a cunningly disguised piece of marketing for a brand of jeans.

SuperGreg
tinyurl.com/5jvd5n

Most Internet crazes are marked by people leaping on the bandwagon, failing to get both feet on it, falling off and bruising their knee on the kerb. At the beginning of this book we reminded ourselves of Mahir Çağrı, the Turkish love machine who unwittingly became famous because of his amateurish homepage; in 2000 Lee jeans capitalized on the public's newly found interest in embarrassing, poorly laid out websites written in stilted English by creating three similar sites – supergreg.com, rubberburner.com and borntodestroy.com. This is the only smouldering remnant of what was a surprisingly effective campaign.

John West salmon ad

youtube.com/
watch?v=zOpKFPEah3E

The product: salmon steaks. The advert: scrapping with men in bear costumes on riverbanks. The outcome: a copper-bottomed viral video hit.

It's fortunate for the human race that we don't have to engage in pitched battle with vicious wild animals to get hold of the ingredients for canned produce. (The baked bean industry must be particularly thankful.) But John West did a good job of convincing us of the lengths to which its employees are prepared to go in order to secure us with juicy salmon steaks – in this case fighting with brown bears on riverbanks. They went on to produce other ads in a similar vein – including people diving over waterfalls and emerging from the belly of a shark – but this was the original, and one of the first widely shared Internet videos.

Evil cosmetics

youtube.com/watch?v=JaH4y6ZjSfE

Dove produced this effective pseudo-political montage urging parents to talk to their daughters (and, presumably, recommend that they use Dove cosmetics) before less conscientious cosmetics companies succeed in brainwashing them into having plastic surgery or embarking on detox diets. The irony of a beauty brand megalith representing itself as some kind of guerilla organization within the beauty industry wasn't lost on some people; one YouTube user pointed out that Dove is owned by Unilever, and that one other Unilever brand in particular doesn't have such a great track record (youtube.com/watch?v=SwDEF-w4rJk).

Marketing and money

While millions of dollars are splurged every month on advertising campaigns, pets.com kept it real with home-produced footage of this sock puppet. The adverts live on long after the original campaign.

Pets.com puppet

youtube.com/watch?v=slCSyC9u5il

Pets.com, an online company that delivered pet food, was one of the most catastrophic dotcom collapses of the late 1990s. But what they lacked in entrepreneurial nous, they made up for with advertising flair: the pets.com puppet – an extremely unconvincing sock-shaped dog stuck on the end of a clearly visible human arm – was way more popular than the company's services ever were. Indeed, the rights to the puppet were snapped up after pets.com's demise, and he's now used to sell car loans. Which is about as absurd as the Sugar Puffs Honey Monster flogging laser eye surgery.

Philips bodygroom

shaveeverywhere.com

The razor business have done to death the idea of shaving closer, to the point where getting any closer would inevitably mean removing layers of skin. So Philips' cunning strategy was to try to persuade its customers to, in the words of the creator of this viral ad, "keep shaving even after they've run out of face". Without recourse to a huge budget, a series of seven straightforward clips demonstrated the value of eradicating every last millimetre of hair from the human body – replacing the rude parts of our anatomy with references to innocuous fruit and vegetables.

"To be or not to be" is no longer the question. "Will it blend" is the question. And the answer is almost always "Yes". From the website you can even click a link to suggest something you'd like to see blended.

Will it blend?
willitblend.com

In the same way that a stapler is assessed on its ability to staple and a computer on its capacity to compute, a blender has to be able to blend. Tom Dickson, the man behind Blendtec blenders, decided to push his brand to the limit by blending stuff that doesn't necessarily need blending, but certainly demonstrates blending power. Golf balls, for example. Matches, marbles, credit cards, soup – still in the can – and, most notably, an iPod and an iPhone. It's got to the stage where no piece of technology has truly proved its worth unless it's been blended to a fine powder by Tom Dickson. And he's shifted thousands upon thousands of blenders as a result.

When viral marketing goes wrong

It's not surprising that, with the amount of resources piled into marketing products on the Internet, occasionally things backfire. No online campaign is ever guaranteed to resonate with the public, but there are two ways that it's possible to pretty much ensure failure: firstly to give the Internet community the idea of taking the campaign into their own hands and producing their own, far less flattering versions; and secondly to pretend that you're not doing a marketing campaign, fail to cover your tracks, and subsequently be exposed to widespread ridicule.

By far the best example of the former is Chevrolet's disastrous campaign for the Tahoe. They teamed up with Donald Trump's *The Apprentice* franchise to create a website that allowed people to make their own commercials – selecting their own backgrounds, video shots and text. On offer were prizes such as a picturesque weekend break or tickets to baseball games, but most people chose to compete for what was, in many ways, a more valuable prize: the recognition of the Internet community in having created the most inappropriate or damning video. Many chose to focus on the Tahoe's gas guzzling engine, but many more were unpublishable in a family book such as this one. Of course, as with many of these campaigns, the results have long since been removed from the Net by panicking PR departments.

You don't even have to screw up an advertising campaign online; the public's irritation with the TV commercials made by a financial services company called Picture Loans have seen a glut of videos on YouTube that either poke fun directly at them (*youtube.com/watch?v=J0qAL1JUSRU*) or simply feature people turning the air purple with colourful language while the commercial plays in the background. While savaging an irritating marketing campaign is an understandable response, it does have the side effect of publicizing the very thing that you profess to hate; Picture Loans are probably delighted at the free publicity.

Nothing, however, provokes the ire of the Internet community more than a site or a blog that masquerades as a consumer opinion site, but is actually written by the product manufacturer. On a small scale, the cloak of anonymity offered by online reviewing has led to authors giving their own books glowing plaudits, and hoteliers recommending their

They claimed that this average-looking blog wasn't an advert for Wal-Mart. I mean, why would they advertise Wal-Mart? But eventually the truth came out.

"charming" premises. But when a multinational is caught at it, they end up having to backpedal furiously. Sony was memorably unmasked as the creators of a so-called "sock puppet blog" or "flog", that featured a teenage boy desperate to receive a PsP console for Christmas. (*youtube.com/watch?v=bwdhg_whoKw*); Wal-mart was also caught out, when its PR company – Edelman – devised a fake blog based around the idea that a couple were driving cross-country and staying only in Wal-Mart car parks. It later emerged that the blog's writer was a photojournalist from the *Washington Post*, and furnished with the vehicle by Wal-Mart. Ouch (*tinyurl.com/6hj6wg*).

But perhaps the most notable misfiring by an advertising company was this excrucaiting pitch (*spike.com/video/2760631*) that Agency.com made for the account of sandwich outlet Subway. They chose to "go meta" by themselves creating a viral video documenting the pitch; it went horribly wrong when the response, instead of being constructive, turned out to be overwhelmingly bile fuelled. One of the phrases in the video – "when we roll, we roll big" – became an ironic metaphor for misguided overconfidence, and another ad firm, Coudal, bit back with this fantastic riposte (*coudal.com/unsolicited.php*).

Matador el café
youtube.com/user/MatadorJoselito

Spanish technology company FON considered all the options they had to communicate the sheer Spanishness of their Wi-Fi routers, ruled out using straw donkeys, paella or Basque seperatists, and plumped for a Net crazy matador who is desperate to get online. He flails his red cloth wildly at passing traffic, sneers at people in Starbucks who are paying through the nose for their Wi-Fi hotspots, and challenges everyone he meets to direct him to the nearest free Internet access point, without success. Of course, his skills as a matador weren't compromised. "If I'm here, don't worry for bulls," he reassures someone tapping away on their laptop.

Bride has massive hair wig out
youtube.com/watch?v=_nFDnC8SSWQ

After intense speculation over whether this video was real (a bride returning from her hairdresser after a disastrous hairdo just minutes before her ceremony), an actress owned up and quietly revealed that it was a viral video produced to promote a range of Sunsilk hair products. Cue widespread confusion: why would you want to establish a link between haircare products and bad haircuts? Why wasn't Sunsilk mentioned? Why wasn't Sunsilk shown riding to the rescue? Why, at the end of the viral, are we still left with a unhappy bride with a bad haircut? Widely viewed, sure – but what was the point?

Whopper freakout
whopperfreakout.com

If you ever needed proof (other than obesity statistics) of how devoted Americans are to their favourite burgers, this video encapsulated it beautifully. Filmed with hidden cameras inside a Burger King restaurant in Las Vegas, this viral showed members of the public freaking out when they were informed that the signature burger, the Whopper, had been discontinued. Some people will, no doubt, have just calmly asked for a Rodeo Cheeseburger instead, but the people in the video react with disbelief, horror, and in some cases blind fury. What better way to celebrate the Whopper's golden anniversary than remind people of its crucial role in the American diet?

Save Karyn

savekaryn-originalsite.com

Karyn Bosnak moved to New York as an ambitious 27-year-old television producer, and immediately spent her way into a $20,000 credit card debt that she could see no way of paying off. So she put up a website asking for donations and, incredibly, cleared the debt in five months. Some saw the website and the inevitable book deal that followed it as a stark warning of the dangers of overspending and the ease with which credit can lead to hideous debt. Others thought that the warning might have been more effective if she hadn't managed to get herself out of trouble by what effectively amounted to begging.

Lower my bills

lowermybillswatch.blogspot.com

LowerMyBills.com is one of the Web's biggest advertisers, splurging millions of dollars in order to persuade us to use its services and save ourselves a bit of cash. Nothing particularly astonishing there – other than the means that is uses to attract our attention rarely has anything to do with finance. It ignores

Marketing and money

several golden rules of advertising by choosing to distract us with incongruous figurines with massive heads, a couple gyrating on a roof, a dinosaur decorated with buttons ... no one quite knows what its strategy is. But they're still around, making bizarre ads. So it must be working.

Orbitz games
orbitzgames.com

Orbitz is just another online travel portal, but its strategy to drag us there and get us to spend money is by deploying arcade games – thus creating the strange spectacle of a travel company with a gaming offshoot. It's a matter of opinion as to whether the kind of people who hang around playing an O-Throw Ring Toss are also likely to splash out on a return flight to Buenos Aires. But Orbitz believe that it's generating an organic community of "Orbitz enthusiasts who will connect with the brand when they are thinking about travel". Anyone for a game of eight ball pool and a holiday in Spain?

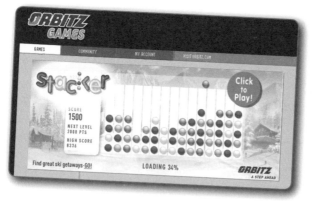

Orbitz let you play Shuffleboard, Airdog, Bean Bag Toss, and the incredibly compelling Stacker. And if you're still in need of diversion, you can click through (as seen bottom-left) to be offered discounted holidays and short breaks ... hurrah!

Lonelygirl15

youtube.com/profile?user=lonelygirl15

It's perhaps not surprising that, in a Web community dominated by shy young men, the appearance on YouTube of a regular video log by an attractive sixteen-year-old girl would attract something of a following. But despite the desperate need those young men had to believe that she was real, as her popularity ballooned so did speculation that there might be a bigger creative force at work. And so it turned out: Lonelygirl was a twenty-year-old actress from New Zealand, whose now unashamedly fictional adventures still have a huge following, and rake in cash for a number of interested parties.

HeadOn

youtube.com/watch?v=ls3icfcbmbs

It's a marketing department's dream scenario: your advert gets picked up by Internet users, forwarded, played, replayed, guffawed at, parodied, reposted and watched millions of times. HeadOn, a homeopathic remedy for headache relief, hammers its message home by repeating, three times "HeadOn – Apply Directly To The Forehead". Not much else happens. In fact, nothing else happens. It's kitsch, it's repetitive, it's mysterious (the advert doesn't state what HeadOn actually does) and strangely hilarious; we may not have thrown out our paracetemol and aspirin, but we definitely love the ad.

Million dollar homepage

milliondollarhomepage.com

Alex Tew, a 21-year-old student from Wiltshire, decided to sell advertising space on his website for $1 per pixel. A simple idea, but surely it could never work. Could it? Sadly, for those of us who dream of getting rich quick, persistently fail to do so and despise anyone who actually manages it, Tew earned over a million dollars for his 1000x1000 pixel page. The plan was for the money to help him pay his way through university; the media attention and subsequent business opportunities ensured that he didn't stay at university for very long.

To you, it might look like the most overwhelming, confusing, poorly designed advertisement ever conceived. But for one Wiltshire student it represented a leap onto the property ladder.

The geek

The Internet is, supposedly, for all of us. Websites are constantly tweaked, reworked and redesigned in an attempt to broaden their appeal, make them easier to use, quicker to navigate and give us the information we require quickly and easily. (Most of the time they fail utterly to achieve this, but that's beside the point.) And now that we're increasingly encouraged to "Have Our Say", people of all creeds, colours and political allegiances have been teased out of the woodwork and into the open, to form a rainbow coalition of Internet users slagging each other off with gusto.

But there's one group of people, geeky *übermenschen*, who'd probably rather we all went away. They like to think that it's their domain. They were around posting on bulletin boards back in 1991 through 9600bps modems. They

The geek

nursed the Internet through its infancy, guided it through puberty and are appalled that several million people have turned up with their Wi-Fi routers and broken up the party with their inane blogs detailing their ectopic pregnancies and endless photos of dull holidays in Silesia. They talk with great sadness of The September That Never Ended (tinyurl.com/67z2dz), the moment in September 1993 when AOL opened access to Usenet discussion groups for all its customers, and suddenly the Internet was visibly rammed with people who didn't know the difference between ROM and RAM and were keen to demonstrate their ignorance in big, shouty capital letters.

This sneering at "newbies" – people who aren't familiar with often arcane Internet etiquette – still goes on, and probably always will. Many geeky types like to construct a jargonized, impenetrable world where everyone outside the clique is made to feel like an outsider, and they're happy to create that supposed utopia in various small corners of the World Wide Web. But, having said all this, we have a lot to thank the geeks for. They've been responsible for the onward push of Web technology, and without them we probably wouldn't even be online. Our favourite websites would be laughably primitive; BBC News would be as pathetic as Teletext, YouTube would be a place where you could read about metal tubes, and Google would only return search results from university dissertations.

And while their technological savvy is responsible for this back-end coding that we never see and that we take very much for granted, they've also created some magnificent Internet attractions – not just ones that only appeal to other geeks, but are lowbrow enough to be applauded by the wider world. So let's put our hands together, ladies and gentlemen, for The Geek.

Mona Lisa with Microsoft Paint
youtube.com/watch?v=uk2sPl_Z7ZU

Having artistic talent is one thing, but demonstrating that artistic talent using a piece of software as rudimentary as Microsoft Paint is quite another. While the luscious graphics you see in magazines are usually generated by high-end software such as Illustrator or Photoshop, Paint is more suited to producing stick figures, badly proportioned dogs, or invitations to Alan's 45th birthday party. This video, however, shows what can be done when it's loaded onto the PC of a true master. To be honest, his *Mona* looks as if she's eaten a few more pies than Da Vinci's *Mona*. But then, haven't we all.

Laptop pizza box
humanbeans.net/powerpizza

Anyone who has to carry their laptop around towns or cities will be aware of how those specially reinforced padding bags we carry them around in tend to scream "Laptop!" before adding, in a shrill soprano, "And that's an extremely portable, high-value, easily stealable item." We could hoik them around in binliners or strap them to our chests in an attempt to disguise them, but here's a more effective, if not elegant solution: the pizza box. "Anti-theft, anti-shock, anti-style," says the website. Just place your laptop in the authentic Italian pizza box, and then keep your fingers crossed that someone isn't looking to steal a freshly made margherita.

"OK, so let me check this: a 15" Apple PowerBook with 2GB RAM, 60GB hard disk, extra pepperoni, mushrooms, and gorgonzola cheese?"

The geek

If you thought that creating pictures using only letters and numbers imposed a needless limitation on the artist, search for "ASCII art" online and prepare to me amazed. And amused.

Star Wars asciimation
asciimation.co.nz

Readers over the age of 35 might remember the days before flashy graphics, when sprites and polygon meshing were the gibberings of sci-fi crazed fantasists. Games on such cutting-edge computers as Sinclair's ZX81 would be constructed from a limited range of symbols – letters, numbers and punctuation – turning a game of Space Invaders into a face-off between some exclamation marks and a descending maelstrom of As and Vs. Retro chic has seen this evolve into an artform known as ASCII art, and its most obsessive practitioners have put together this version of *Star Wars*. I guess that someone, somewhere, is reworking *Shrek* into tapestry format.

Back yard roller coaster
jeremyreid.com

Some dads might, say, suspend an old tyre from a metal frame in order to give their kids something to swing on. Few would attempt to construct Jeremy Reid's miniature theme park, not least because of the absence of a relevant "Help Sheet" in their local DIY superstore. Unimpeded by inquisitive health and safety officers, Reid put together a rickety looking 450-foot rollercoaster track in his admittedly enormous back yard, made out of "pressure treated southern yellow pine". If Michael Jackson ends up having to sell Neverland, maybe Reid could help him downgrade.

Like being struck by lightning, but in reverse: Dr Megavolt makes electricity simultaneously fun and dangerous.

Tesla coils
drmegavolt.com

We prefer electricity to stay within insulated wires, quietly powering food processors and nasal hair trimmers without exploding into a violent flash of light and carbonizing our earlobes. But within a controlled environment, watching electricity can be fun! Well, Dr Megavolt certainly thinks so: his childhood fascination with tesla coils (transformers which have the ability to "shoot electricity into the air") has regularly led him to don a protective suit and give night-time displays of shooting lightning bolts back and forth with his bare hands. Another enterprising soul has used tesla coils as a musical instrument, albeit one that you don't want to get too close to (youtube.com/watch?v=B1O2jcfOylU).

Lego

It's Ole Kirk Christiansen's fault. He was the Danish wooden toy maker who started the Lego business back in the 1930s and who, in 1949, began to produce the interlocking plastic bricks that are now strewn across the planet: six hundred pieces are manufactured every second, and there are enough Lego bricks in circulation for every human being to have a pocketful of 62 (which would probably hurt quite a lot whenever you tried to sit down). There's an extraordinary enthusiasm for Lego online, a passion bordering on reverence. It has the unusual characteristic of being beloved of both children and geeks, of being simultaneously cutting-edge, kitsch and retro. And it's that mass appeal that not only fires people up to produce such outlandish Lego creations as a Macintosh computer (*tinyurl.com/68rjlf*), a working harpsichord (*tinyurl.com/abooe*), a lie detector (*tinyurl.com/obd4g*) and a crossbow (*tinyurl.com/zveoj*) but also drives people in their hundreds of thousands to go to these websites and take a look.

While building models of things – however unconventional they may be – is still seen as the purest form of Lego related fun, this often requires a level of technical know-how that some people can't be bothered to acquire. And those people might instead channel their creativity into vignettes; these are defined at *vignettebricks.blogspot.com* as "a scene built of Lego bricks on a small (usually 6x6 or 8x8) base". These vignettes might be from history, from film or television, but more ambitious vignetters have taken things to a whole new level. Sci-fi buffs will swoon at Legostar Galactica (http://*legostargalactica.comicgen.com*), a comic strip built with Lego, while Irregular Webcomic (*irregularwebcomic.net*) tackles issues from British quarantine laws to the ferrying of the newly dead across the River Hades via the medium of small plastic bricks. Perhaps the most popular, though, is

If your creative limits with a Lego set are constructing a rickety, multi-coloured house with mis-shapen windows, open your eyes to the distinctly sci-fi-lookin' Legostar Galactica.

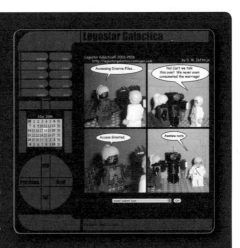

The Brick Testament (*www. thebricktestament.com*) in which Brendan Powell Smith stages Lego scenes from the Good Book. And, if that weren't already irreverent enough, he superimposes suitably un-Bible-like thought bubbles above the main protagonists. There have also been a number of spin-off books that probably don't go down very well at Christian fundamentalist dinner parties.

The obvious extension of vignettes is stop motion animation. The Lego Group were doing this back in the 1980s, but once again the boom in online video sharing has given anyone with a Lego set and a camera the ability to reconstruct Eddie Izzard comedy sketches (*youtube.com/watch?v=Sv5iEK-IEzw*), indulge in the "bricksploitation" of Monty Python (*youtube.com/watch?v=fIXByCAlzos*) or make a Lego viral of the OK Go treadmill video we mentioned in Chapter 2 (*youtube.com/watch?v=DjCL0_0Il7w*). The Lego Group has, of course, scored great successes with its computer games featuring Lego characters, but they move so smoothly that, ironically, it feels a bit unrealistic. What the online community seems to prefer is to "keep Lego real", by reducing a game as slick as Grand Theft Auto to the status of a primitive home-made animation (*youtube.com/watch?v=ThxpAIZzXXo*).

It might remind you of a wall of glass bricks, but the Tenori-On is one of a new breed of musical instruments that you don't blow, pluck or hit.

Tenori-On

youtube.com/watch?v=_SGwDhKTrwU

Music technology tends to come in instantly recognizable formats – either a keyboard with knobs, or a black box with knobs. Imagine the delight of musicians worldwide when they were suddenly presented with a new toy that looked like an oversized glittery drinks coaster and had none of the usual controls; you just seemed to prod at it and wait for interesting noises to emerge. This video shows a demo performance from someone clearly involved in making the thing. This one, however (youtube.com/watch?v=_SGwDhKTrwU), shows what happens when someone gets frustrated with its idiosyncracies.

Powerbook chime

prangstgrup.com

For some, the computer startup chime is a glorious sound, an affirmation that everything is okay within and that your precious data hasn't been irretrievably mangled. For others, it's a grim precursor to another tedious working day. For people in a quiet library trying to study, however, it's always profoundly irritating – especially when one chime in particular has been extended over a minute and a half, like some kind of hideous new age symphony, purely in order to wind them up as part of a student prank. It makes you wonder if startup chimes are necessary at all. (Conclusion: no, they're not.)

Ways of making students in lecture theatres spontaneously applaud: a) announce the introduction of a campus-wide "free beer" policy, or b) fill a fishtank with some sulphur hexafluoride and float objects on top of it.

Invisible water effect

youtube.com/watch?v=tAsOfqCy4A0

This short film shows a couple of scientists demonstrating that the gas sulphur hexafluoride has similar properties to water, in that it can be poured from one vessel into another and objects can float on top of it. Of course, the implications of this aren't particularly profound for mankind; you'll never be able to irrigate deserts or replenish reservoirs with the stuff, and popping out to sulphur hexafluoride your garden won't have any noticable effect. But put the stuff in a tank in a lecture theatre and the results are undeniably impressive.

Baseball batting robot

baseball-bats.net/robot

This specially built robot, which can detect an incoming baseball and thwack it away with a mechanical swipe, shows how future sporting events might well be pitted between man and machine. Forget the chess computer Deep Thought; people will crowd into arenas to see the boxers of the day attempt to inflict damage on a robot made of some kind of titanium alloy, while the winner of the US Open tennis tournament won't actually have a name, but will come with a 13-digit serial number, an instruction manual and a back-to-base 24-month warranty.

Cockroach-controlled mobile robot
conceptlab.com/roachbot/

This student has managed to push back the frontiers of, well, terror, by plonking a live Madagascan hissing cockroach onto a trackball wired up to a robot with wheels, and allowing it to use its almighty power to weight ratio to manoeuvre the vehicle. While the point of the project was to help secure a master's degree, it raises all kinds of sinister questions – mainly related to the cockroach being placed in a position of power. Who knows what these creatures could achieve. They're terrifyingly robust, they've got plenty of time at their disposal, and they have no sense of guilt or shame. May the Lord have mercy on our souls.

Breakfast TV nuclear explosion
youtube.com/watch?v=MzaN2x8qXcM

Nothing is more likely to put you off your muesli than witnessing a sudden nuclear explosion while watching live footage from the roving weather camera on breakfast TV. Fortunately, for those watching *Česká Televize* that morning, these images didn't indicate imminent war with Poland; rather that a guerrilla artist collective known as Ztohoven had hacked into the camera and inserted the mushroom cloud footage in order to wake up the Czech Republic a bit more smartly than usual. Six members of the collective ended up facing prosecution for the prank, despite it winning them a national prize for young artists.

Chain reaction
youtube.com/watch?v=U82eWptFxSs

If you search for "Chain Reaction" on YouTube, you'll inevitably find Diana Ross at the top of the page. But look a bit further down, and you'll find this 1987 art project by Peter Fischli and David Weiss, which features not quite as much kooky 1960s-style shimmying, but quite a few more tyres, seesaws, ramps and explosions. This five-minute video is part of a full thirty-minute film of beautifully choreographed chain reactions between inanimate objects, moved along by fire, water, gravity and chemistry. It's like that kids' board game Mousetrap, except a bit more likely to leave you with burns and slight bruising.

Christmas lights gone wild
youtube.com/watch?v=rmgf60Cl_ks

People used to be willing to travel for miles in order to watch Christmas light displays in city centres. These days, however,

The geek

amateur electricians prefer to set to work and create home-made lighting spectaculars worthy of Jean-Michel Jarre. Ohio resident Carson Williams used sixteen thousand lights in his 2004 creation, which presumably had the knock-on effect of causing sleepless nights among neighbours, traffic congestion, litter, and plummeting house prices in the immediate vicinity. But on YouTube, well, it's nothing short of magnificent.

24: **The unaired 1994 pilot**

collegehumor.com/video:1788161

Go on, try running a counter-terrorist unit with technology that's fifteen years out of date. Not particularly easy, is it? In this fantastic spoof of *24*, Jack Bauer has to safeguard America from terrorist threat equipped only with a pager – which requires him to take time consuming and dangerous trips to the nearest phone booth – and an AOL account via a noisy 28.8kbps modem. Back at CTU headquarters, Nina Myers is unable to get a file over to Jack because it's too big – three floppies! "Just print it out and we'll send a bike messenger," says George Mason, leaving Nina to wrestle with an uncooperative dot matrix printer.

Collegehumor.com was once just a little project started by two high school kids from Baltimore; today it's one of the premier sources of original sketch comedy on the Internet.

Non-Newtonian fluid
youtube.com/watch?v=f2XQ97XHjVw

The scientific definition of a Non-Newtonian fluid is a fluid whose viscosity is variable based on applied stress. But there's a way to demonstrate this that doesn't require you to reach for your chemistry text books; just fill a small pool with water, add a load of cornstarch, and walk across its surface in a Messiah-like fashion. This being the Internet age, our experience of the phenomenon has been shaped by this particular clip, which is Spanish in origin and exhibits all the clichés of European TV – i.e. pulling stupid faces and screaming. There's not much point in watching past the 1.20 mark, unless you're a glutton for punishment.

Head tracking with Wii
youtube.com/watch?v=Jd3-eiid-Uw

The Wii Remote is an astonishing piece of equipment: its built-in accelerometer allows me to swing a virtual tennis racquet in exactly the same hamfisted way I do in real life. But while some hackers were trying to get the device to work with non-Nintendo games, one American student, Johnny Chung Lee, put its infrared capabilities to more intriguing uses. "Head tracking for virtual reality displays" might not sound very interesting, but just watch this video, and you'll see how it'll radically change computer gaming. If this hasn't already secured Jonny a job at Nintendo, their recruitment department must be in a coma.

Angry German kid
youtube.com/watch?v=kBVmflUR1DA

Don't worry, this is a fake. In fact, it's so obviously a kid messing about that it's incredible that the clip was ever taken seriously.

MIT hacks

Students, eh. You've got to love their crazy, lovable antics. On the other hand, you might loathe their smug, alcohol fuelled, desperately unamusing attempts at practical jokes, like the time they filled your sleeping bag with banana flavoured yoghurt, or the occasion when they shaved off your eyebrows when you were asleep, formed the hair into a moustache and sellotaped it onto your favourite Debbie Harry poster. Or when they rang your mum at midnight to tell her that you were dead. Fortunately, you get a better class of student than this at Massachusetts Institute of Technology, according to the long-established website at http://*hacks.mit.edu*. While hacking is synonymous with someone gaining access to your credit card details via some insecure backdoor on your PC, MIT hackers are, according to their FAQ, people who do "some sort of interesting and creative work at a high intensity level, from writing computer programs to pulling a clever prank that amuses and delights everyone on campus". So why are they featured here, and not with all the practical jokers back in Chapter 3? Because the sheer ingenuity of many of the pranks immediately elevates them to honorary geek status. This lot wouldn't bother filling your sleeping bag with banana flavoured yoghurt, unless it involved making the yoghurt from scratch, and getting it into the sleeping bag by a process of osmosis.

While *hacks.mit.edu* has become the natural online home of these pranks, many of the stunts date back as far as 1984, a time when recording every single aspect of each hack in infinite detail just wasn't possible – or, even if it was, it wasn't deemed important to do so. So for some of the hacks we can only read the description, sit back and imagine what it might have been like – for instance 1991's "Great MIT Hack Talk". Brian Leibowitz, a former MIT student, was delivering a talk in a large lecture theatre, but unbeknownst to him students had rewired the audio system and patched the signal from his microphone through a pitch shifting unit. As the talk progressed, Liebowitz's voice rose, at first imperceptibly, but eventually enough for his giggling audience to realize what was going on. His status as a hacking victim finally became clear to him at the point where he started to sound like a cartoon character.

If you ever need to know how to get a police car on top of a university building, your should probably start your enquiries with students at the Massachusetts Institute of Technology.

Okay, so that's a pretty simple rewiring job, but the "Green Building VU Meter" was something far more ambitious. To coincide with the 4 July celebrations in 1993, students turned the top floor of one of the campus buildings into the world's largest VU meter – some 250 times the size of the one flashing away on your hi-fi at home. The meter was linked to the live radio broadcast of the Boston Pops, giving a real-time VU display across the city. And then there was the electronic construction sign near the MIT campus, which was hacked to give the following information to passing motorists: "Massachusetts Ave Bridge Closed ... Sunday 04/22/07 6am-3pm ... To Appease Godzilla." Nice. Here are a few more highlights: the firehose turned into a drinking fountain (h*acks.mit.edu/Hacks/by_year/1991/fire_hydrant*), elevators that suddenly gain the power of speech (*hacks.mit.edu/Hacks/by_ year/1998/talking_elevator*) and a campus police vehicle, pictured above, that was somehow placed on top of MIT's Great Dome (*hacks.mit.edu/Hacks/by_year/1994/cp_car*).

The geek

What's more interesting is the back story: that the boy in question produced the video as a parody of what many believe is the effect of videogames on children: their minds ravaged by attention deficit hyperactivity disorder, reducing them to screaming little imbeciles. He put it online, only to see it splashed across the media as an example of, er, what videogames can do to children. Sadly, the boy mistook confusing a load of gullible Internet users for thespian flair. "I have acting talent," he stated, tragically.

Lasse Gjertsen
youtube.com/watch?v=JzqumbhfxRo

As an idea, it's simplicity itself. Musicians have been messing about with cut, paste and copy techniques for years, snipping a single drum hit and reusing it to form the backbeat of a song. Emboldened by forward strides in home video editing technology, Lass Gjertsen took it one step further by using the same technique, but using footage of him amateurishly smacking a drum kit. In doing so he created a video beatbox, deliberately unsophisticated but undeniably original. Since then it's been much copied in the world of advertising, notably by Volkswagen.

You might think that a stack of advanced musical technology will compensate for your lack of musical skills, but you still need to have a great idea – and Lasse Gjertsen's video cut-up techniques turned out to be inspirational.

Human Tetris

notsonoisy.com/tetris

Only an artist could experience that leap of imagination necessary to see an empty theatre, picture each seat as a pixel on a computer screen, and set about recreating classic computer games by getting people in coloured t-shirts to sit in particular seats. Guillaume Reymond has, at the time of writing, created four such masterpieces using stop motion animation (notsonoisy.com/gameover) but the one that immediately grabbed attention online was his Tetris game (pictured above), which involved 88 human pixels, 880 seperate pictures and, no doubt, a whole load of standing up and sitting down.

Anyone who has ever had sleepless nights imagining coloured blocks coming towards them will identify with Guillaume Reymond's Tetris-based art project.

How do I shot web?

tinyurl.com/2mqnaw

It's impossible to sum this up any better than wikichan.org: "How Do I Shot Web originates from a question posed by a gamer on GameFAQs.com asking how to make his in-game character shoot webbing; the poorly worded phrase was then Photoshopped onto an image of a baffled looking Spider-Man. The meme saw a surge of popularity following 9/11, where jumpers falling from the doomed towers were shown to be imploring Spider-Man to tell them how to "shot web", to which his reply was "I dunno lol." ("I dunno lol" is now considered the only proper reply to "How do I shot web.")

Leeeeroy Jenkins
youtube.com/watch?v=LkCNJRfSZBU

I don't really understand why anyone would want to play World Of Warcraft, wasting precious hours fighting battles in an alternate reality while the potatoes boil dry or the bath runs over. But this is still incredibly funny. A mock-up of a WOW battle scenario, it features a group of players earnestly discussing battle strategy in an area known as the Blackrock Spire, when one of their number, Leeroy Jenkins, interrupts the discussion by shouting "Let's do this! Leeerooooy Jeeenkins!" and rushes in ahead of the pack to face certain annihilation. Suicidal behaviour in online gaming has henceforth been known as "pulling a Leeroy".

CounterStrike cheat
youtube.com/watch?v=nwF1zGrNril

This video was made back in 2001 as a promotional clip for a LAN party – an event where hundreds of people descend on a venue with their computers and play hour after hour of network based games against each other. Someone is accused of cheating, and instant justice is dispensed by an angry mob that ejects him from the venue and smashes his computer into tiny pieces. Of course, people immediately thought it was real, forgetting that the last thing anyone engaged in network gaming would do is to actually get up from their chair. Even if their own mother was on fire.

Be warned: Mentos mints react explosively with Diet Coke to produce a delightful fountain effect – so don't try it at home.

Actually, go ahead, try it at home – everyone's been doing it since EepyBird.com's experiments were posted online.

Mentos and Diet Coke
eepybird.com

This is every kid's dream scenario. Let loose in the kitchen, you'd love to discover two ingredients which, when combined, react against each other violently, explode messily and leave the breakfast bar covered in an unappetising sludge. While Fritz and Stephen – who comprise EepyBird – weren't the ones to discover that Diet Coke and Mentos have such a aggressive antipathy towards one another, they are most definitely the ones who brought it to the masses via the Net, and went on to create shows in London, Paris, New York and Istanbul that fired minty jets of sugar-free fizz several hundred feet into the air.

All your base are belong to us
tinyurl.com/eyoyr

Poor translations into English are always funny, whether they are hanging on the back of the door of a hotel room, on a Chinese menu or, indeed, in the opening sequence of a Sega

Mega Drive game called *Zero Hour*. The basic message just about gets across (that there's an imminent threat from alien lifeforms – a well-worn gaming scenario) but the alien chooses to convey this fact by saying "All Your Base Are Belong To Us", before rounding it off with a decidedly unsinister "ha ha ha". The sequence was expanded into this mash-up video which quickly became the king of all geeky Internet memes.

The parlour

youtube.com/watch?v=Ge2FHDf_L78

The stultefying boredom of Internet chatrooms is perfectly recreated in this fantastic short film, along with their creepiness, perversion, inanity and excessive swearing. And, crucially, it puts faces to the screen names, from the thirtysomething schizo who voices fantasies of mass murder, to a middle-aged woman, "Bambi", who just doesn't get it and who everyone is desperate to ignore. It's beautifully acted and has a superb punchline based on that common scenario of two men chatting together online, with one (or both) of them pretending to be women. Not something that Tim Berners-Lee, inventor of the World Wide Web, would ever have seen coming.

Timewasting

Not so long ago, successful parenting seemed to be based around sternly turning off the TV and forcing children to go outside and do something more constructive – like butterfly collecting, perhaps, or kicking a ball around in a local park until it was stolen by the bigger boys. Who knows, before the advent of television, maybe these activities were themselves deemed a frivolous, unbeneficial waste of time. But what goes around comes around and, now, after fifty years of allowing to suck up the greater part of our leisure time, our ardour for the gogglebox is rapidly cooling. Instead, we've transferred our affections to the Internet, a mistress far more compelling and irresistible than TV could ever have hoped to be.

Timewasting

This whole book is, to some extent, about wasting time. No immediate, discernible benefit comes from watching a rock band lark about on treadmills, or studying a cartoon approximation of a cat playing a guitar. Aside, maybe, from that brief, ephemeral moment of pleasure we seem to get from these links, that in turn persuades us to go and seek out another brief, ephemeral moment of Web related pleasure. It's a rapid downward spiral.

So, how to combat our addiction to the websites that are particularly alluring? Readers of stronger moral fibre might say "Just turn it off!" or "Use a bit of will power!" But frankly, many of us are too feeble, and too easily led astray. We need help. And that's what an almost biblical sounding bit of software called Temptation Blocker was designed to provide, by preventing certain programs launching on your computer within certain time frames, unless you type a very annoying and unmemorable 32-character password. But obviously, if you've installed the software, you can probably work out how to uninstall it. My own preferred procrastination buster is to set up my computer to emit a loud "CLANG" every twenty minutes to remind me that I might well be wasting my life on some non-essential Internet diversion. Invariably I am, and the "CLANG" orders me straight back to work.

But occasionally we want the Internet to take us away from it all, to help us forget, to occupy our minds for several hours at a stretch while the phone rings off the hook and the bath overflows. Many links we've already looked at have this capacity, of course. But this collection of immensely popular sites has particular potential to reduce your life to a meaningless sham, set to a soundtrack of random mouse clicks on a permanent loop. Be warned.

Bzzzpeek

tinyurl.com/3wycw

If you've ever been desperate to hear a Korean person attempt to do a passable imitation of a sheep, Bzzzpeek offers you an unmissable opportunity (via dogs emblazoned with flags no less).

Should you ever find yourself slightly drunk in a bar in a foreign land and fancy striking up some kind of rapport with the locals, here's a quick recipe for an instant bonding exercise. Draw a rough sketch of a pig, point at it, and say "Oink oink". They will collapse in hysterics, and reciprocate with their own pig noise which, if they're Hungarian, will be "Rurf rurf". Then you will collapse in hysterics, order another beer, draw a bee and say "Bzzzz", and they'll collapse in hysterics and say "Zoom zoom". And you will collapse in hysterics, order beers for everyone in the bar and then pass out. This website is a bit like that.

Let them sing it for you

tinyurl.com/57xuxm

This project by a Swedish artist called Erik Bünger allows you to deliver messages to people made up of individual syllables from some of the world's best known pop songs. Yes, of course it's pointless, but isn't most of the Internet? So a phrase as mundane as "Listen. I am going to the shops. Would anyone like to come with me?" is represented by an unholy collision of Depeche Mode, Chris Isaak, Bing Crosby, Shakespeare's Sister, UB40 and a whole load of other artistes that zipped by too quickly to be identified. Dubious from a copyright point of view, but probably frivolous enough to escape prosecution.

Timewasting

Springs, pulleys, girders and gravity collide – almost literally – in SodaConstructor, an engrossing virtual construction tool.

SodaConstructor
tinyurl.com/3h2s4a

In the hands of an engineer or someone with an advanced qualification in Applied Mathematics, this Java-based tool might conceivably have some useful real world function – I dunno, assisting them in the construction of a perpetual motion machine, or solving the ancient conundrum of "why is air?". For the rest of us, it's just a cute toy with which we can draw a load of lines on a screen, connect them with springs, and then subject the whole thing to gravity (or anti-gravity) before erasing it all, starting again and wondering what on earth we were supposed to be doing with our afternoon.

Scrabulous
apps.facebook.com/scrabulous

For many people, the social networking site Facebook would be a lot less popular if it wasn't for this unauthorized version of Scrabble, created by two Indian brothers, Rajat and Jayant Agarwalla. There's been a lot of um-ing and ah-ing over its legality, but at the time of writing it's still online with over six hundred thousand users desperately wishing that QAJAX was a word. It not only contributed to a resurgence of interest in Scrabble, but also to an unprecedented boom in views of anagram-solving websites, which help to increase one's chances of winning via that noble method of cheating. And anyone who says they don't use them is lying.

Cheddarvision
cheddarvision.tv

Watching cheese mature isn't like watching paint dry. It's worse. A thin layer of gloss emulsion is safe to touch within a few hours, but this piece of cheddar – which was viewed by over 1.5m people on its very own webcam – took a year to mature, and shaved precious minutes off the lives of all who bothered to look at it. Affectionately named "Wedginald" by its manufacturers, it was bought by a winery in New Zealand, spirited across the globe, and now has its own rather less popular website at whereswedginald.tv. If you'd like to see its year in the spotlight in a time-saving minute-long video, see youtube.com/watch?v=KXMYF7xPD7A.

I WAS A STAR ONCE YOU KNOW

Can you really be addicted to the Internet?

If you've got this far in the book, you could probably class yourself as an Internet addict, albeit a reasonably well adjusted one. I'm the same. I check email eagerly. My Internet enabled phone is used far too frequently to settle disputes in bars over which actors played various 1970s sitcom characters. But a woman called Dr Kimberley Young doesn't just believe that we're addicted to the Internet. She figures that we need help, and urgently. Her investigations into so-called Internet Addiction Disorder (IAD) have led to a book, *Caught In The Net*, which presents "the stories of dozens of lives shattered by a compulsion to surf the Net". Her website, The Center For Internet Addiction Recovery (*netaddiction.com*) contains a wealth of highly compulsive reading material which allows you to spend several hours browsing and listening to podcasts to determine whether or not you actually have a problem. "Do you block out disturbing thoughts about your life with soothing thoughts of the Internet?" asks her Internet Addiction Test; score too highly, and online counselling is recommended at $95 per hour. Meanwhile, Dr Ivan Goldberg, an ally of Dr Young, has developed a list of symptoms of IAD, ranging from the mundane and familiar – "Internet is accessed more often than was intended" – to terrifying cold turkey scenarios: "tremors, trembling, involuntary typing movements of the fingers".

But before you rush to the phone to make an appointment with your GP, there's an equally vociferous group of psychologists who consider the theory of IAD to be deeply flawed, and that thinking about it too much merely creates needless worry. And I'm kind of on their side. If you're online, you're mainly reading or writing. And if you were sitting quietly reading a book or writing a letter, no one would be telling you that you have some kind of disorder. Of course, addiction to online pornography or online gambling has its own methods of treatment, but as of now, Internet addiction itself isn't a recognized psychopathology, appearing in neither of two internationally recognized handbooks for diagnosing mental disorders – although the likes of Dr Young are lobbying hard for it to be included.

So okay, you might spend too much time online, but then again you might also argue with your partner, eat too many all butter croissants or have lustful thoughts about minor celebrities – but these things can't really be ranked alongside schizophrenia or depression. There's just something about finding an updated page or a new snippet of information that gives a momentary pleasure. Surely we can't be denied that? And there are dozens of people who I'd never have met without the Internet, and there's no way that the time I spend communicating with them online can possibly be deemed unhealthy. But if you're not reassured, and you're worried about Dr Young's concerns, there's a simple method of self-assessment: just try not using the Internet for a week. And if you can make it through those seven days without at least a twinge of longing, well, you're made of sterner stuff than I am.

Find of the day
foundmagazine.com

If a comprehensive social history of the human race ever comes to be written – and can I make it clear at this point that I'm not volunteering – it's not the blogs, the autobiographies, the diaries that will shed most light on our behaviour. It's the stuff that was never meant to be seen: the dark secrets penned in old notebooks, the surreptitious pieces of paper passed between people at work, the private albums of Polaroids. These reveal what we really thought, what we really got up to; *Found Magazine* has recognized this, and created the most fascinating trove of documents that have been discovered in the attics, under the floorboards and lining the cutlery drawers of ordinary people.

SheepShooting
tinyurl.com/45ddg

Reaction tests are horribly addictive. As it's a test of instinct rather than skill, everyone thinks that they can beat their sluggish personal best, and everyone's prepared to spend a long time doing so. It's a pride thing; deep down we'd like to think that if a fluffy kitten ran out in front of our moped, we'd slam on the brakes within a fraction of a second and save the little mite from imminent destruction. But sadly, it's not always the case. This BBC flash game measures how fast you react to a sheep dashing across the screen before you can press a button to tranquilize it. My best score was 0.19 seconds, but bear in mind I could be lying just to look good.

Wasting time on the Internet has never been as relaxing as those dreamy minutes spent in the company of FlyGuy.

FlyGuy
trevorvanmeter.com/flyguy/flyGuy.swf

This is a marvellously relaxing way to spend half an hour. You just manoeuvre a slightly balding, pixelated, airborne chap around the scrolling screen, encountering various objects and people as you go. There's no aim as such, no chance of meeting a sticky end; just the pleasure of exploring an off-kilter world that exists only in the mind of the designer, Trevor Van Meter, while gently picked acoustic guitars chime away in the background. If more video games were like this, there'd be fewer hyperactive kids and a lot more would-be philosophers.

Copter
hurtwood.demon.co.uk/Fun/copter.swf

"Just one more go," you think to yourself after about 45 minutes. "I can't let this elementary dexterity test show me up. If I can't manage to manoeuvre a virtual helicopter through a green cavern, what hope do I have behind the wheel of a car?" Thing is, when you're driving a car there's the odd moment of relaxation. Occasionally you can pull up at a red light, or have a teabreak in a layby, or drum your fingers on the wheel while you sit in stationary traffic on the Paris ring road. But in this game, if you lose a fraction of a second of concentration, you're done for. About as emotionally exhausting as a divorce.

Online Spirograph lets you create those familiar symmetrical patterns without recourse to pen, paper, pins and patience.

Spirograph
tinyurl.com/334fjv

Kids don't know they're born, these days. Back in the 1970s all we used to have to amuse ourselves was a set of coloured pens, a range of clear plastic pieces with small teeth, and sheets of paper on which we'd create flowery symmetrical patterns. Actually, I don't know why I sound bitter – I loved Spirograph. And I used to pine after Super Spirograph, advertised on the back of the Spirograph box, which enabled you to, I dunno, split the atom or something. Here's the online equivalent, which pushes all the right buttons from a design perspective, but loses some of the inherent magic of wrestling with Spirograph's leaky biros.

Can you cope with the stress of someone preventing you spelling out a message using virtual fridge magnets? The answer is probably no, but it's worth having a try.

Fridge magnets
tinyurl.com/6mj4pk

If proof were ever needed that it's impossible for people to work together in complete harmony, just unleash them on a virtual fridge door with a few dozen virtual fridge magnets, and watch them sabotage each other's attempts at laboriously spelling out messages. It's a weird one, this. There's absolutely nothing to it, but it sucks you in and keeps you there for hours, achieving nothing, learning nothing, observing very little of note. The most tragic message I saw was "I should be writing the next chapter of my book". And it wasn't even me that wrote it.

Webcams of the world
opentopia.com/hiddencam.php?showmode=animated

It's a collection of the most mundane webcams in the world, but curiously fascinating. Under typically tedious footage of AutoEcosse Motor Sales in Dundee, a chap called "Lightning Fox" has posted a comment: "Fantastic cam! You can see the cars and people buying them!" There's another set up in the main square of Most, a town in northern Bohemia. A band I was in once played in a bar in Most in 1993. There was barely anyone there. There's barely anyone visible in Most's main square on the webcam, either, so my theory that my band was magnificent and Most is actually a ghost town is finally gaining a bit of weight.

Google earth
earth.google.com

Google Earth provides aerial pictures of the globe, giving you a satellite's eye view of country lanes, waterfalls, volcano craters, and consigns any small titbits you may have learnt on time management courses to the waste bin of history. Sites such as googlesightseeing.com suggest that many people do little else other than cruise around the planet from the comfort of an office chair, unearthing such oddities as the Lancaster bomber flying over Huntingdon (tinyurl.com/9xl3z) or the forty-metre profanity carved into a field outside Billingley, Yorkshire (tinyurl.com/aftv2) – while Google Street View adds a whole other voyeuristic dimension (tinyurl.com/65lbyk).

Ugly people
uglypeople.com

This is the polar opposite to that similarly addictive website hotornot.com. But while the latter lures you in with images of people who apparently consider themselves to be attractive in some way, and have posted their smouldering poses in order to have that confirmed by the wider Internet community, uglypeople.com is just a hideous gallery of the follically, nasally or dentally challenged. Or, in some cases, all three. You might think it's cruel to rate people from one to ten according to how ugly they are, but hey, at least no one has put them in a booth at a circus. As far as I know.

Jelly battle
jellybattle.com

It's only after you've spent a significant proportion of your morning making jelly babies jump around the screen and melt each other with space age laser beams that you actually spot that this game was created by Logitech (manufacturers of computer peripherals) and, actually, you've spent all morning being subliminally persuaded to go out and buy a Logitech product. I've got a Logitech mouse right here to prove it. It's a shame that I'm so easily brainwashed but, on the other hand, I did get to control a load of massive laser-equipped jelly babies. Three cheers for capitalism.

Notpron adventure
deathball.net/notpron/notpron.htm

Adventure games have moved on from the old text-based format, where you'd type in simple commands ("look west", "crack nut", "disregard furniture") and the computer would offer up unhelpful responses ("I don't know how to disregard the furniture"). These days, traditional adventure games are generally deemed a bit old hat; modern gaming does, of course,

Timewasting at work

Imagine for a moment that, in a rare show of generosity by your boss, you were given an assistant. A fantastic, efficient assistant who never once argued with you, was never off sick, never questioned your decision making processes and did exactly as you told them. But also happened to be intriguing, knowledgable – somehow beautiful. You fell in love with them. You couldn't take your eyes off them. You just sat there, staring at them for hour after hour. Your productivity slumped alarmingly. Eventually, you were told that you couldn't have your assistant any more. From now on, they'd be seated in a seperate office, and you'd only be allowed to talk to them at lunchtime. Ring any bells?

According to those who profess to know best, as the Internet has become a standard office tool over the past five to ten years, office workers have become way more productive than they used to be. But you try telling that to your boss when he's just hauled you in for an embarrassing disciplinary at which you're presented with irrefutable proof of your dodgy surfing habits. Did you really spend an hour reading about the drinking habits of Canadian snooker star Bill Werbeniuk? Yes, I'm afraid you did. While you should have been revising the provisional marketing budget. You're fired.

Aimless Internet browsing during the average working week accounts for, on average, 3.9 hours of office time – equating to over two hundred lost man hours every year per employee. Many people will look at these figures and snort with laughter from behind their hands, fully aware that they get through those 3.9 hours of timewasting in a single working day, never mind a whole week. So it's not surprising that companies use services such as Message Labs and Clearswift to monitor our online activity. The IT department will tell you that this is because of network security (social networking sites in particular are known to carry links to dodgy pages containing malware) and to cover their backs legally. But at the same time, if you spent two hours sucking up data from webcams in Lithuanian brothels, it's pretty unlikely that this will go unremarked upon by your supervisor.

A couple of years back, one company attempted to turn this shameless timewasting at work to the advantage of businesses, by creating special company search pages that employees would use; these pages would carry advertising, and any revenue derived from clicks on the company search page would be ploughed back into the business. The major flaw, of course, is that you'd be relying on your own workers to click on banner adverts and buy stuff, rather than knuckle down and complete those Powerpoint presentations. Needless to say, the company in question is no longer trading.

But it's tricky to establish that happy medium between the online slacker and the happy, productive employee. Wholesale blocking of websites by companies leads to a miserable workforce, depressed that they no longer have the opportunity to exchange occasional messages with their friends on Facebook, or indeed complete a three thousand-word blog entry about their unreciprocated feelings for the girl who works upstairs in Human Resources. But allow employees to police their own activity, and give them unrestricted, unmonitored access to the Internet? You may as well send them all on holiday. Because while the Internet has undeniably speeded up all manner of processes at work – research, fact checking and of course communicating – you can bet your life that the time saved by the Internet has also been squandered on the Internet.

involve a certain amount of problem solving – it's just combined with slaughtering as many lifeforms as possible. This one, however, requires a bit of "thinking outside the box". If you can't get past the second screen, you're probably better off sticking to Pacman.

Falling sand
chir.ag/stuff/sand

Four streams of sand sprinkle from the heavens, their progress gently guided by a series of obstructions that you carefully draw on the screen using a range of specially provided tools. When someone creates a relaxing Internet attraction such as this, you fear it might be a setup for a gag where a toothless crone suddenly appears on the screen peeling off her skin to frighten you half to death (see Maze Of Concentration, p00). But there are no surprises here. Just sand. Endless streams of sand, interacting with each other in a benign, inoffensive way. Perfectly safe for children, although they may start to cry out of sheer boredom.

Something awful
somethingawful.com

Most Internet users have their own favourite forums, where they spend hours exchanging strongly held opinions with one another and eventually invoking Godwin's Law ("As an online discussion grows longer, the probability of a comparison involving Nazis or Hitler approaches one"). But would they fork out $9.95 for the privilege? Probably not. Something Awful has managed to harness a secret ingredient that not only keeps around a hundred thousand people coming back for more, but also prises money out of them for the privilege – almost unheard of in this freeloading Internet age. Respect due.

Here we have a man with an enormous neck playing a banjo, while a mandolin and acoustic guitar patiently await their turn on his knee. You'll find rotten.com to be full of such glorious spectacles.

rotten.com
rotten.com

In the next chapter we'll look at a whole load of things that you wish you hadn't seen on the Internet. But for the time being, rotten.com is a perfect timewasting destination if, say, you feel a bit queasy when you see a picture of a lovable kitten playing with a ball of wool, but you don't feel remotely troubled when browsing through images of criminals being hanged in the Ukraine in the late nineteenth century. You've never seen so much injury, death and general unpleasantness as there is on rotten.com. And, as the cliche goes, it's like a car crash. You just can't take your eyes off it, despite wishing you could.

The omnificent English dictionary in limerick form
tinyurl.com/y7guwa

What better way to enhance people's understanding of the English language than to place its individual words into limericks? Actually, several ways spring to mind – but that doesn't make this any less of a valiant project, if heroically pointless. With over 42,000 approved limericks in its searchable database, covering a range of topics from astrology to statistics, there's a good chance you'll come away slightly amused, if none the wiser. Modern Physics is worth a browse: "The factory simply called 'B', makes very expensive debris, with positrons gnashing, electrons, it's smashing, out mesons with 6 GeV." Boom-boom.

How to be the perfect girlfriend
tinyurl.com/y6l2mg

"Life Explained. On Film." is the Videojug's strapline; quite why "How to be the perfect girlfriend" is always amongst the most viewed video clips is something of a mystery – especially since the tongue-in-cheek advice it dispenses consists mainly of how to indulge said boyfriend's whims to the point where he'd become an egotistical, power-crazed maniac. But amongst the site's enormous stash of how tos are such indispensable instructions as how to avoid a trapped arm while hugging your partner, how to make Kadhai Paneer, how to tie a full Windsor knot and, fittingly, how to upload an instructional video to Videojug.

Wayback machine
archive.org

Not everyone has realized that everything you ever publish on the Internet is likely to be archived somehow, somewhere. And it may resurface in a few years' time, providing undeniable proof that you had a habit in 2002 of going online late at night while extremely drunk and professing your undying love for your cognitive behavioural therapist. The Wayback Machine is one place where you can reach back in time and dig up things that their creators hoped had long since bitten the dust. It also provides a reminder of how far Web design has come on; try comparing tinyurl.com/579wm5 with bbc.co.uk…

Weboggle
wordsplay.net

Here's another word game – in this case Boggle – that has found itself online in a massively popular, but unofficial version. But while a game of Scrabulous is a leisurely, laid-back affair that can take a week or more of gentle pondering to complete, Wordsplay is utterly relentless. As soon as you've been thrashed to within an inch of your life by some twelve-year-old language genius from Saskatchewan, you've got scant seconds to regain your composure before the next game starts. As one friend with a haunted, desperate look on her face once said to me: "That website is like crack."

Help to create misery for millions of children worldwide by using the Sober Santa game to get Father Christmas monumentally drunk.

Sober Santa
tinyurl.com/yzdo9n

There are thousands upon thousands of diverting Flash games on the Internet. But as programmers master the format, they seem to be trying to make things more complicated – you know, multiple screens, extensive arsenals of weaponry operated by various key commands, and a gaming scenario that you need a weighty booklet to explain properly. This, however, is more like it: simply manoeuvre a Santa figure around a roof, picking up glasses of champagne, which slowly render him unresponsive to your desperate stabbing of the arrow keys until he finally slides off. Simple, beautiful, festive.

Line rider

tinyurl.com/23rmjs

Boštjan Cadež, a Slovenian university student, hit upon the brilliantly simple idea of getting the gaming enthusiast to, er, construct his own game as well as play it. Rather than provide a pre-determined slope for his little cartoon tobogannist, Cadež lets us draw it, press go, and see how the little fellow copes with our improbable slopes. If you get the hang of it, you can see him power his way through several thousand feet of trouble-free winter sports (youtube.com/watch?v=bcu8ZdJ2dQo). If you're like me, however, you'll see him fall off almost immediately and perish from exposure. The game was recently bought by a bargain hungry gaming company; console versions are, apparently, imminent.

Stranger than fiction

Before the Internet existed, our experience of eccentric behaviour was limited to dealing with a dotty great aunt's compulsion to hide packs of frozen sausages behind nests of occasional tables, or watching hyperactive fitness instructors squealing with misplaced enthusiasm on breakfast television. We had no idea that, for example, somewhere in the UK a woman was attempting to wean her child off breast milk by drawing monstrous faces around her nipples using felt-tip pen. The information wasn't ever passed in our direction. How could we have found out? Certainly not by watching television or reading newspapers. "There's only so much unusualness the public can take,"

media moguls might well have mused. "If they know the truth, that absolutely everyone is exhibiting erratic, unusual behaviour on a daily basis, civilization as we know it will just crumble. Let's just give them a weather forecast."

Now the truth, as they say, is out there. The Internet draws bizarre and inexplicable weirdness out of the woodwork like the chime of an ice cream van brings children scurrying into the street. It's likely that people have always been making gateaux out of minced beef. It's almost certain. It's just that they were unable to let us know. But now we're so swamped by online eccentricity that the bar has inevitably been raised; a video of someone balancing a ballet pump on their nose while reciting Paul's *Second Epistle to the Corinthians* wouldn't even raise an eyebrow. The weird are having to outweird the weird in order to grab the tiniest sliver of our attention spans. But here is a collection of some of the fruitcakes that have either proudly risen to the top of the Internet heap, or simply been unable to slot conveniently into any other part of this book. File under unfileable.

Speed painting with ketchup and french fries
youtube.com/watch?v=1gvGDslYrrQ

"My medium is clay," a sculptor might say. A cake decorator, if pressed, might admit to her medium being marzipan. But few internationally recognized artists have ever created a meisterwerk from McDonald's fries and ketchup. In this four-minute video (thankfully condensed from fifty minutes for all us time poor timewasters) we see the artist create an image of

Morgan Spurlock (of *Super Size Me* fame) using fast food. In fact, it's the same chap who created the *Mona Lisa* using Microsoft Paint in our Geek chapter, but he deserves two entries just for his stubborn refusal to use a paintbrush like any normal person.

English Russia

tinyurl.com/35zfkg

This site is devoted to bringing us sublime nuggets of stupidity from the Russian-speaking online community – things that we'd never normally discover because of Russia's stubborn insistence on having its own language and alphabet. This post uncovers a Russian photo challenge, budding photographers are presented with the following scenario to recreate: "A man ('the lover') hangs out of a window wearing only red underpants. Another man leans out from another window, aiming a gun at 'the lover'. From yet another window 'the cheating wife' looks out in despair." Marvel at how life and limb are risked to provide us with a fleeting moment of amusement.

Roy Orbison in clingfilm

tinyurl.com/a8yi

Erotic fanfiction, also known as slash fiction, has a perfect home on the Internet. Most people won't share your perverted fantasies about the drummer of Fleetwood Mac, and won't bother reading them. But if some people do, you can collaborate feverishly on a Fleetwood Mac orgy scenario. Ulrich

Haarbürste, however, only has eyes for one person, and that's Roy Orbison, as long as he's wrapped in clingfilm. His collection of seven stories, in which the situation delicately but tortuously unfolds to leave Roy wrapped head to foot in PVC, are a wonder to behold. Sadly, Ulrich himself is the fictitious brainchild of one Mr Michael Kelly, but that doesn't make the stories any less gripping.

The Berlin Wall – a love story
berlinermauer.se

Eija-Riitta is a Swedish woman who describes herself as Objectum-Sexual; in a nutshell this means that she feels a powerful, passionate attraction to inanimate objects. There are advantages to Objectum-Sexuality: your partners are unlikely to cheat on you, offend your mother or rifle through your underwear drawer. But when Eija-Riitta married the Berlin Wall in the late seventies, she could never have predicted the events of the evening of 9 November 1989; for many the fall of the Wall was a joyous occasion marking the end of the Cold War, but for Eija-Riitta it was just a mob setting about her defenceless husband with sticks.

Amy Grant's mandible
tinyurl.com/6yg3ac

Amy Grant is, apparently, the best-selling contemporary Christian music singer on the planet. As an atheist with an aversion to acoustic guitars, I've never heard of her, but still. Thirty million people have delighted in her God-fearing ditties, but one person has a more specific reason for becoming a fan: the shape of her lower jaw. "It kind of juts out, as if Amy's gritting her teeth or something." This is the story of how the author persuaded a friend to get Amy's autograph and compliment her on her mandible; even more bizarre are the featured emails from people who think they're actually writing to Amy Grant (tinyurl.com/6283ys).

Steve, don't eat it
tinyurl.com/3owts

During a stroll through an average supermarket, you're likely to see hundreds of products you might not be happy putting in your mouth. (I'm not talking about stuff in the toiletries section; that hopefully goes without saying.) Cheese string, canned potatoes, those pork pies with a hard-boiled egg suspended in the middle… Steve from The Sneeze blog, however, has spent four years unearthing the most unappetizing groceries imaginable, and then making a point of eating them so we don't have to. Pickled pork lips, silkworm pupae and mouldy sweetcorn are all digested – if not with relish, then certainly with bravery.

If you've never had mouldy sweetcorn for dinner, but have a burning desire to find out what it might be like, allow Steve from The Sneeze blog to fill you in.

Singing ponies
tinyurl.com/2d8m

If you've ever dreamt of being a conductor, of wielding a baton in front of a hundred musicians as they respond with flawless musicianship to every movement of your hand, while a thousand people behind you wonder why on earth you're

I really wish I hadn't seen that

You might like to think that you're as broadminded as the next person, but on the Internet you really have no idea who the next person could be. They might think nothing of knocking up a quick home video of themselves defacating into a bowl, garnishing it with parsley, wrapping the mixture up in clingfilm, taking it into a local park, throwing it into the air and smacking it incredibly hard with a baseball bat. But the thoroughly unhygenic scenario I've just outlined is nothing compared to the horrors awaiting you in certain darkened corners of the Web. As an adult, you probably never consider activating parental controls or children's filters when you're using the computer. You probably figure that you can deal with whatever the Internet can throw at you. But there are some inexplicably popular Internet virals that you really ought to be gently steered away from.

We're not talking illegal content, here. (Although, as you'll no doubt be aware from news stories regularly splashed across the media, there's a lot of that awaiting you, too – if you're stupid enough to look for it – along with a hefty prison sentence if you get caught.) No, these are just pictures or videos of adults going about their everyday business. It just happens to be the kind of everyday business that would make most normal people try and rip out their retinas in a futile attempt to erase the image from memory.

This presents us with the tricky problem of telling you about the most popular webpages that you wish you'd never seen, without actually encouraging you to go and have a look. Because you know how it is: your inbuilt curiosity will get the better of you, you'll casually do an Internet search, see something you really wish you hadn't seen, and then write a furious email demanding to know why Rough Guides is publicising such filth. I must confess that I've actually seen none of the below; I'm horribly squeamish, so while I've read accounts of what they're about and seen grown men flinching at the memory of them, I've managed to avoid them completely. So it can be done. Just don't look. Some people have. Millions have. But they nearly all wish they hadn't. So don't look. Just don't.

Don't look at the video of a girl eating a live mouse. It's not big, it's not clever, it might not even be real, but don't look. Don't follow the link from the Wikipedia page about Bud Dwyer, the American politician who committed suicide live on TV. Don't watch anything called SWAP.avi, and be very wary of any file called hello.jpg. Don't watch the video of the man appearing to cut off a rather integral part of his body; I've not given you enough information for you to find it, but don't even try to look for it. Similarly, the picture of a girl attempting some kind of anti-grav toilet manoeuvre in the bath. Forget I even told you about it. By all means join the millions who have delighted in the "reaction videos" of people experiencing some of these monstrosities – Kermit The Frog's is a good one (*youtube. com/watch?v=nOn1htjSZic*) – but never, ever, ever attempt to look at the originals. You'll never forgive youself. And you'll only have yourself to blame.

Stranger than fiction

It's a barbershop quartet, but not as we know it: the Singing Ponies waiting to be prodded into action.

waving your arms about, well, you can break yourself in gently with the Singing Ponies. Click on a pony, it'll start singing. Click on another pony and it'll start humming. Click on them again and they'll stop. Marvel as your mouse clicks build a staggering cathedral of sound. Seriously, it's just like the Berlin Philharmonic.

Eric conveys an emotion
emotioneric.com

A young employee of Yahoo! by the name of Eric decided that his gift to the world would be to take pictures of himself enacting various emotions as dictated by his audience. And, against the odds, he found an audience willing to tell him what to do. It's kind of like the Subservient Chicken we saw at the beginning of the book, but actually done to order, and without the subtext of trying to sell burgers. Eric has successfully demonstrated love, panic, pity and sexual arousal (I can actually do those four at once) while his "to do" list includes schizophrenic joy, arachnophobia, losing a lottery ticket and allergy to vertical blinds.

Harder, better, faster, stronger: a fiendishly complex hand-jive that presents palm-penned subtitles of the track's lyrics. This clip brought Daft Punk fans and finger fetishists together for the very first time in History.

Daft hands

youtube.com/watch?v=K2cYWfq--Nw

Had the person behind Daft Hands hawked their act around the talent scouts of Broadway in the late 1940s, they'd have been met with a quizzical stare, a shout of "Next!" and a swift ushering out of the nearest fire exit. But it was always going to be cheap to stage: no special effects necessary, no performing animals or fireworks. Just two hands, a biro, and a tape of the Daft Punk song "Harder, Better, Faster, Stronger". So it was done at home, in one take, with a single camera, and the resulting video succeeded in being nine times more popular on YouTube than Daft Punk's original. You're unlikely to see Daft Hands doing a sell-out run at the London Palladium, but it's still a classic of the genre.

Randy Constan

pixyland.org/peterpan

Peter Pan, the boy who wouldn't grow up, was able to soar magically through the air by using a potent combination of happy thoughts and fairy dust. Randy Constan has not, as far as we know, hurled himself off a building in order to test his powers of flight, but in all other ways has attempted to emulate his hero. Green tights, check. Feather in green cap, check. Leaping about a lot, check. Despite his florid language, love of tearjerkers and keenness on being a pixie, a fairy or an elf, Randy is, against all the odds, a fiercely heterosexual chap. And indeed found the love of his life, Dorothy, via his jawdropping website (tinyurl.com/2ub8w6). Brace yourself.

Meat was never designed to be worn as a hat, but there's no rule that says you can't give it a go. And they're not afraid of experimenting at hatsofmeat.com.

Hats of meat
hatsofmeat.com

We're embarking on a meaty trilogy, now. Many people are appalled by the slaughter of animals for food, so the slaughter of animals for amusing headgear will probably drive them to take militant action against the creators of this website. From the skullcap made of the finest Canadian bacon to the famed brisket yarmulke, Hats Of Meat does exactly what it says in the address bar; anyone wishing to sport their own meat hats would be best advized to beware of hungry dogs (a water pistol filled with lemon juice will help) and the Animal Liberation Front (a water pistol filled with lemon juice will have little effect).

Stinkymeat
stinkymeat.net

Anyone fascinated by the way meat decays should probably consider some kind of scientific career developing food preservatives, but while they're swotting up and gaining the necessary qualifications, this website will provide a certain amount of distraction. Mahlon Smith, in a moment of curiosity, bravado and boredom, decided to leave a plate full of meat to fend for itself in his neighbour's back yard. Just to see what would happen. The ensuing stench and arrival of local insect life was documented in repellent detail for thousands upon thousands of interested but appalled viewers.

A delicious gateau with a savoury surprise in store: it's constructed from meatloaf and mash.

Black Widow bakery
tinyurl.com/mgouh

This starts out as a fairly unremarkable "online baking/patisserie portfolio", with some cakes, a few chocolates and a braided loaf. But an online baking/patisserie portfolio does not a viral Internet sensation make – until, that is, the baker in question decides to make a beautifully decorated cake entirely out of meatloaf, with mashed potato icing and ketchup glaze. It looks like a dessert. But it's really a main course, to be served hot. Ugh. "How did it taste?" asks an inquisitive fan of the Meatcake. "Like meatloaf and mashed potatoes," comes the slightly bemused reply.

Stranger than fiction

Alex Chiu
alexchiu.com

Alex Chiu has succeeded in unravelling the mysteries of life where centuries of the world's finest scientists and philosophers have failed. And what's more, he's happy to share with us the benefits of his wisdom: just $123 will secure you a pair of foot braces, a pair of Neodymium Immortaility Rings and one bottle of "Gorgeouspil" (so-called because they're pills, and they, er, make you gorgeous). Alex has the solution to a unified world, everlasting life and world poverty, but can't seem to work out why his website doesn't appear on the Google search engine. "Google is afraid of Alex Chiu," he says. "Tell others about Alex Chiu." Okay: Alex Chiu will help you stay beautiful for eternity. Barring any nasty accidents, of course.

Fireworks up ass
youtube.com/watch?v=33PnwYpXgf8

Of all the places you might consider placing a lighted firework, "in my rectum" would have to come almost at the bottom of the list – perhaps nudging ahead of "in my mouth", but still several thousand places below "attached to a stick buried firmly into the ground, well away from crowds of human beings and not pointing towards the heads of small children and vulnerable animals". Incredibly, no ill effects were suffered as a result of this pointless experiment, although if the man in question ever decides to stand for political office, this moment may come back to haunt him.

Chuck Norris facts
chucknorrisfacts.com

Chuck Norris can divide by zero. If you can see Chuck Norris, Chuck Norris can see you. There is no theory of evolution, just a list of creatures Chuck Norris has allowed to live. If you have five dollars and Chuck Norris has five dollars, Chuck Norris has more money than you. You get the idea, right? Let's play… Chuck Norris can make an omelette without breaking eggs. Chuck Norris can fly without any kind of mechanical aid. Chuck Norris can construct a triangle given the lengths of its three bisectors. I could go on, but I won't.

At last, the opportunity to dress up your goose as a human being. What's that? You don't have a goose? Hey, that's not going to be a problem at geeseclothes.com.

Geese clothes
geeseclothes.com

It's hard to know where to begin with this one. I know of no one who has a model goose. If I did know someone with a model goose, I'd hope that they kept it in the attic rather than put it on display. If they dressed up the model goose, I'd start questioning my friendship with them. If they regularly changed the outfit in order to align the goose seasonally with various public holidays, I'd urge them to seek help. But here's a website for that very purpose. And alarmingly, if you don't have a model goose, they offer a range of plastic, resin or concrete geese in order to help you embark on an exciting new hobby.

Love's great adventure

Before the Internet got in on the act, the rigmarole of finding a suitable partner would consist of either a) being introduced to someone ridiculously inappropriate at a specially arranged and excruciatingly awkward dinner party or double date; b) hanging around in bars or nightclubs in the vain hope that Mr or Mrs Right would walk through the door and not be put off by your desperate, lascivious, drunken leering; or c) taking the socially unacceptable step of joining a dating agency, and trying to ensure that no one you knew ever found out how desperate you were.

But the Internet has made the speculative, match-seeking date not only acceptable, but a popular and efficient way of finding someone who might put up with all your little idiosyncracies. While journalists used to turn out dozens of articles to tell us of their incredible adventures in the world of online dating, we no longer need them to tell us what it's like, because most of us know: it's magnificent when it works, and soul destroying when your date "goes to the toilet" after five minutes and then fails to reappear.

While most people choose to cast their net as widely as possible on the biggest online dating sites, others head for more unusual or specialist pools of people, in order to fulfil their requirements for, say, a seven-foot ballroom dancing enthusiast from Swaziland. The "miltary singles and emergency services" dating site at *uniformdating. com* presumably caters for those who'd like their date to turn up in fatigues or a hard hat, and carrying a whistle. Meanwhile, *datemypet. com* improves your chances of meeting your true love by using your dog, parrot or terrapin as some kind of personality decoy. Those who don't trust themselves to assess someone's suitability accurately could try out *parship.co.uk*, which matches you with people based on a psychometric test, or maybe you'd prefer *astralhearts.com*, which puts you through a spiritual profiling exercise and then presumably steers you away from any Leos or Sagittarians.

Mysinglefriend.com relies on your friends writing your profile for you, so it's worth keeping your fingers crossed that they don't tell the story of the time you vomited into your previous partner's slippers, while *beautifulpeople.net* is probably the most nerve-racking site of them all, because unless you conform to certain aesthetic standards your profile will be rejected by the existing users of the site before you've even had a chance to get going.

More enterprising people might set up their own website in an attempt to seek out a beau; Allan Wills travelled the globe looking for someone who'd be prepared to marry him, blogged about it (*areyoumywife.com*), eventually found a woman called CeCe, transplanted the blog into a book, and then started another blog to recount their courtship (*ourultimatedate.com*). Which some people might find excessive, although in the desperation stakes it's still better than the man who's offering a reward of $10,000 to the person who introduces him to his future wife (*10k4awife.com*).

Of course, finding a date online is basically about lying. Or, at the very least, lying by omission and seeing if you manage to get away with it. And the spoof dating site PoorMatch manages to satirize the whole business beautifully, although I would say that because I helped to write it (*tinyurl.com/5mkrhl*). "We met online and literally within seconds we were regretting exchanging mobile phone numbers and email addresses. Thank you, PoorMatch!"

Sudanese man forced to marry goat

tinyurl.com/hnto3

Without having the statistics to hand, I'll stick my neck out and say that this is the most viewed story on the BBC News website. Just when you think you'll never see it again in the "most emailed" or "most viewed" list on the site, it'll inevitably crop up – just like Slade seem to every Christmas when "Merry Xmas Everybody" hovers into the lower reaches of the singles chart. Who knows why we're so titillated by the story of a man caught having sex with a goat and subsequently forced to marry said goat by the village elders. Perhaps it's a case of "there but for the grace of God go I".

Ridiculous black metal videos

tinyurl.com/5qsw6f

When I was eleven I remember being scared of goths. They seemed other-worldly … menacing … harbingers of doom. Twenty-five years on, I realize that they're just feeling a bit low and have too much time on their hands. This magnificent video (removed from YouTube, but valiantly preserved here) shows eight hilariously po-faced groups of men made up to look like corpses and charging around forests with guitars, along with two spoofs. (If you can spot the spoofs, you're a better man than I.) Morbid Anal Fog also sends up the genre (youtube.com/watch?v=Qvsq6_8Hzo8) and there's more fun to be had with black metal photo shoots (youtube.com/watch?v=aGZmh2eo8g4). Fingers crossed that these bands don't condemn me to be disembowelled by ghouls and buried in a shallow grave.

Rap music doesn't require extensive graphical and statistical analysis. But that doesn't mean that it's can't be funny when someone does it.

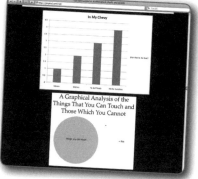

Rap represented mathematically
jamphat.com/rap

There was a recent fad for representing the lyrics of songs using Powerpoint presentation slides and putting them online – you know, like "Analysis of what seems to be the hardest word", or "Flow chart to determine whether you find Rod Stewart sexy". This site was probably the first to attempt this noble endeavour, focusing specifically on rap and containing such triumphs of the overhead projector medium as "Debt Balance for Biggie Smalls Tax Year 1993/4" and "Percentage of boys brought to the yard by respective milkshakes". Groundbreaking work.

Biscuit classification
tinyurl.com/5ru7hq

The question of whether Jaffa Cakes should be classified as cakes or biscuits has tested the finest legal minds in Britain, or certainly some legal minds, at any rate. That's because arcane Value Added Tax laws dictate that the tax is applicable to chocolate covered biscuits, but not other kinds of biscuits, or indeed cakes. McVities, the makers of Jaffa Cakes, believe they are cakes, because they go hard when they're stale. A biscuit would go soft, of course. (I hope you're following this.) Anyway, what the case really required was someone to analyze it using cladistics, whatever that may be, and this webpage is the inexplicably popular result.

Real ultimate ninjas
realultimatepower.net

When I was twelve years old, I'd probably have nominated *The Incredible Hulk* or *The A Team* as the beings that wielded colossal power. These days, though, it's ninjas that grab the male pre-teen imagination. This parody of boyish enthusiasm for precision violence sailed rather predictably over the heads of other young ninja fanatics, who sent furious emails pouring scorn on the site's inaccuracies (such as "I heard that there was this ninja who was eating at a diner. And when some dude dropped a spoon the ninja killed the whole town.") A spin-off book explored in greater detail the peculiar world of the adolescent ninja obsessive.

I LIEK MILK!!!!!!!!
generation.nl/~hitoshi

The phrase "I LIEK MILK" shouldn't throw up anywhere near as many matches on a Google search as it does, but there you go; if nothing else, it provides proof of how the content of a ridiculous Internet viral consisting of a Japanese milk fanatic can somehow enter the online lexicon. People started "lieking" all kinds of stuff following this page's surge in popularity; I've been unable to dig up any details on the guy, whether the page is a joke (I imagine so), and what may have happened to him post-viral fame. But as he claims to drink four pints of milk a day, my guess is that he's in hospital having kidney stones removed.

The Matrix ping pong viral took table tennis from being a three dimensional game to being an extremely bizarre three dimensional game.

Matrix ping pong
youtube.com/watch?v=-dcmDscwEcl

While shows like *Britain's Got Talent* and *America's Got Talent* continue to serve up a series of heavy-footed clog dancers, ungainly acrobats and over-made-up teenage girls warbling medleys from *Phantom Of The Opera*, the Japanese get to see a more inventive talent show, called *Kinchan and Katori Shingo's National Costume Competition*. Judges pronounce their verdicts on various skits, which seem to combine the faking of cinematic special effects with kabuki theatre. This hugely popular video crosses the famous "bullet time" shots from *The Matrix* with a game of table tennis. It probably wouldn't make Piers Morgan or Simon Cowell blub into man-sized tissues, but that's surely to its credit.

Rice field art
vill.inakadate.aomori.jp

Farming is a tough enough occupation, you would have thought, without having to go to excessive efforts in order to make your fields of crops look aesthetically pleasing to anyone peering out of the window of a passing aeroplane. But in one part of rural Japan, different varieties of rice are planted in carefully thought-out patterns, so pictures of waves, mountains, scary-looking mythological figures and the *Mona Lisa* will

emerge at harvest time. ("Doesn't the latter contravene copyrice law?" asked one wag on a page discussing the art.)

Why do people always choose the Mona Lisa to show off their artistic prowess? Japanese farmers give their paddy fields the Da Vinci treatment.

Balloon bowl skating

youtube.com/watch?v=QN_r9joWNXQ

Here, someone manages to identify a sensual pleasure that the human race had hitherto been unaware that it was missing out on: the sensation of feeling balloons rebounding off your face as you skateboard through a skatepark full of them at breakneck speed. Videos of people being pushed down tubes lined with the finest cashmere, or playing catch with hardboiled eggs while standing barefoot on a sheet of Egyptian cotton with an incredibly high thread count are, presumably, in the pipeline.

Reading on a dream

youtube.com/watch?v=-mUyvaPtsJw

The public's attitude towards musical theatre is ambivalent at the best of times, and in some cases can cause violent antipathy. Not least because songs tend to kick off at incredibly inappropriate moments in the plot, like when someone has just been sentenced to fifty years in prison for committing multiple murders ("Violence Is Golden") or been diagnosed with a terminal illness ("Surely You Jest, Dr Best?"). Or, indeed, when everyone is sitting very quietly in a library. Prangstgrup gets away with the latter by injecting some joyful exuberance into an otherwise tedious afternoon of study.

Chucking cans
youtube.com/watch?v=H4alsp1Leol

While the video in chapter 4 of two guys catching sunglasses on their faces was quickly exposed as an admittedly ingenious bit of camera trickery, this video of people casually tossing cans into waste bins from impossible angles and over implausable distances looks more like the real deal, albeit after hours of painstaking rehearsal, filming and editing. Although how the can chuckers managed to keep their happy-go-lucky demeanour after dozens if not hundred of failed attempts, I'm not quite sure. So maybe it is a fake, after all.

Dancing baby
tinyurl.com/ljr9p

One of the oldest Internet virals, Dancing Baby is also one of the creepiest, and certainly not one that you'd particularly want to revisit on the grounds of aesthetic merit – despite the technological wizardry used to achieve it. We're used to seeing our toddlers stumbling around the living room, falling face first onto the carpet or into soft furnishings, and certainly not gyrating provocatively like some backing singer in Earth Wind and Fire. Which might explain why it made us feel so uneasy and, at the same time, remain so memorable.

Bas Rutten street defence
youtube.com/watch?v=D3K-mrlYG7Y

Self-defence always looks easy when someone else is demonstrating it. And the more vicious, sinewy, aggressive and wild-eyed the demonstrator, the easier they make it look. Here, Ultimate Fighting Champion Bas Rutter talks us through a number of manoeuvres, in which he shows us how to smash the heads of various willing actors into upright posts, how to break their arms, crush their cheekbones and steal their lunch money. Crucially, none of the actors bother fighting back (although, looking at Bas, who could blame them?), making it a fairly unrealistic and one-sided exercise in annihilation.

Great Yarmouth waxworks
youtube.com/watch?v=Z7f8RwweCYc

Email inboxes throughout the world were given a rare slice of East Anglian culture back in 2003, when still photos taken at the Louis Tussaud's House Of Wax became the latest forwarding sensation. Rather than an appreciation of artistic skill, however, this was more of a game of Guess Who?; these waxworks are renowned as the worst in the world, bearing only a passing similarity to their subjects. Princess Diana looks more like an aging piano teacher, David and Victoria Beckham look like malnourished bikers, and the less said about Kylie Minogue the better. The notoriety the attraction gained as a result ensured its longevity; some five years later it's still very much open for business.

Le Breton Gourmand
youtube.com/watch?v=41mOnF-9v6E

I think it's only fair that, for the last but one link in the book, I'm allowed to include a contribution of my own – a celebration of the cuisine of northwestern France, which I discovered on some obscure late night cable channel. Sadly, it hasn't racked up tens of thousands of views, but it's surely only a matter of time. The show is in French, but it's overdubbed by French actors who recite a terrifyingly literal and hilariously deadpan English translation, with mundane exchanges about beurre blanc or snails transformed into incredible carnivals of language. I'm not laughing at them, I promise; I just adore it, in the same way one is overcome with delight when a Japanese hotel invites you to "take advantage of the chambermaid".

Last page of the Internet
shibumi.org/eoti.htm

So here we are. The last page of the Internet, supposedly. Those of us who, in our more anxious moments, feel utterly swamped by all the media the Internet foists upon us might like to cast our minds back into history, and to the British scholar Robert Burton. As well as writing the first ever study of depression – *The Anatomy Of Melancholy* – he is supposed to have held the distinguished honour of having read every book that had ever been written. Those were the days, eh. If it were possible to sit poor old Robert down in front of Yahoo!, he'd probably burst into floods of helpless tears and immediately start working on *The Anatomy Of Melancholy II: Electric Boogaloo*.

The Internet isn't infinite, mainly because there isn't an infinite number of hard drives connected to it. But the data that comprises it is expanding so fast and changing so rapidly that even powerful search engines have trouble keeping track of it all. We even have trouble staying on top of the meagre handful of bookmarks that sit oppressively in the menu of our browser. So it may as well be infinite, as far as you or I are concerned. And while it's not difficult to find out what the first page on the World Wide Web was – a series of not particularly thrilling text links uploaded by Tim Berners-Lee (tinyurl.com/3apuu) – the last page, or indeed the most recent one, will already be old by the time our brains have finished processing the concept of the last page of the Internet. Which is why umpteen pages, including this one, make a gag out of it.

Stranger than fiction

"Congratulations! This is the last page. Thank you for visiting the End of the Internet."

It might represent something of a relief to see these words on the screen in front of you. As if you've been winched by some benevolent helicopter out of the swirling mass of information and entertainment you were thrashing around in, and deposited safely on a nearby mountain top. But you know, don't you, that it'll be scant seconds before another video of a kitten or a fat bloke lipsyncing to a Judas Priest song will be spinning, with grim inevitability, in your direction. You can't escape. The Net's got its claws into you. And your only crumb of comfort is that, well, at least some of it is funny. And at least other bits of it are fascinating, eye-opening and informative. It's just a question of filtering out the rubbish. We've done our best in this book. But for now, just savour the fantastic and totally misguided notion that you've seen it all. As the Last Page Of The Internet says:

"There are no more links. You must now turn off your computer and go do something productive. Go read a book, for pete's sake."

(But probably not this one, or you'll be right back where you started.)

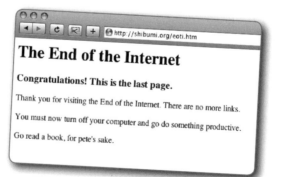

The End of the Internet

Congratulations! This is the last page.

Thank you for visiting the End of the Internet. There are no more links.

You must now turn off your computer and go do something productive.

Go read a book, for pete's sake.

Picture credits

The Publishers have made every effort to identify correctly the rights holders for the use of the images in the book. If for any reason any attribution is incorrect the publishers will correct the error on subsequent reprints once it has been brought to their attention. Front cover, Crazy-Frankenstein.com; inside front cover, Elliot Elam; back cover, Peter Buckley; 11, YouTube.com; 15, Weebls-Stuff.com; 19, YouTube.com/Askgeriatric.com; 20, YouTube.com; 21, YouTube.com; 22, Peter Buckley; 23, Peter Buckley; 25, Peter Buckley; 26, YouTube.com; 27, Guygoma.com; 28, YouTube.com; 32, Elliot Elam; 33, Wherethehellismatt.com; 35, Peter Buckley; 39, YouTube.com; 40, YouTube.com; 41, Elliot Elam; 43, Hitch50.com; 45, YouTube.com; 46, YouTube.com; 47, YouTube.com; 48, YouTube.com; 49, Peter Buckley; 51, Imovie; 54, Dooce.com; 60, Peter Buckley; 61, Ifyoulikeitsomuchwhydontyougolivethere.com; 62, Pearson Asset Library/Dave King (c) Dorling Kindersley; 65, Elliot Elam; 66, Amirtofangsazan.Blogspot.com; 69, Harvardsucks.org; 70, Winterrowd.com; 73, video.google.com; 74, Neistat.com; 75, Elliot Elam; 79, YouTube.com; 80, Elliot Elam; 83, YouTube.com; 85, Snopes.com; 86, Rense.com; 91, Zapatopi.Net; 92, Paul Guinan/Bigredhair.com; 94, Genochoice.com; 96, Theonion.com; 99, Peter Buckley/Wired.com; 101, YouTube.com; 102, Pcworld.com; 104, Icanhascheezburger.com; 105, Faildogs.com; 106, Peter Buckley; 107, YouTube.com; 109, Creativecommons.org; 110, Rathergood.com; 111, Pimpthatsnack.com; 114, Leekspin.Info; 117, Beedogs.com; 118, YouTube.com; 119, YouTube.com; 120, Pearson Asset Library/Dave King (c) Dorling Kindersley; 121, YouTube.com; 123, Pearson Asset Library/Tracy Morgan (c) Dorling Kindersley; 124, YouTube.com; 125, Peter Buckley; 126, YouTube.com; 127, Peter Buckley; 128, Neopets.com; 130, Scalzi.com; 131, YouTube.com; 132, Infinitecat.com; 133, Catsthatlooklikehitler.com; 137, Trojangames.co.uk; 138, Stillfree.com ; 139, Elliot Elam; 141, Peter Buckley; 142, Dreamland.Anshechung.com; 144, Web.Archive.org; 145, YouTube.com; 146, YouTube.com; 147, Willitblend.com; 149, Disobey.com; 152, Orbitzgames.com; 154, Milliondollarhomepage.com; 157, Humanbeans.Net; 158, Asciimation.Co.Nz; 159, Drmegavolt.com; 161, Legostargalactica.comicgen.com; 162, YouTube.com; 163, YouTube.com; 164, Elliot Elam; 166, Collegehumor.com; 169, Hacks.Mit.Edu; 170, YouTube.com; 171, Notsonoisy.com; 173, Eepybird.com; 177, Flat33.com; 178, Sodaplay.com; 179, Peter Buckley; 181, Elliot Elam; 183, Trevorvanmeter.com; 184, Wordsmith.org; 185, Lunchtimers.com; 187, Peter Buckley; 191, Rotten.com; 193, 2flashgames.com; 197, Englishrussia.com; 199, Thesneeze.com; 200, Elliot Elam; 202, Svt.Se; 203, YouTube.com; 204, Hatsofmeat.com; 205, Blackwidowbakery.com; 207, Geeseclothes.com; 209, Theinternetnowinhandybookform.com; 211, Jamphat.com; 213, YouTube.com; 214, Vill.Inakadate.Aomori.Jp; 218, Shibumi.org.

Index

Index

Index